Shiprock, Navajo Reservation, New Mexico.

Desert varnish on wall, Waterpocket Fold, Capitol Reef National Park, Utah.

AMERICAN SOUTHWEST

Navajo weaver, Monument Valley, Arizona.

Dunes and Monument Valley, Navaho Reservation, Arizona.

AMERICAN SOUTHWEST

A PEOPLE AND THEIR LANDSCAPE

Sheep and herders in Monument Valley, Navaho Reservation, Arizona.

WRITTEN BY MICHAEL GRANT, PHOTOGRAPHED BY TOM TILL, PRODUCED BY MCQUISTON & PARTNERS

THUNDER BAY PRESS, SAN DIEGO

CONTENTS

Above, petroglyph, Monument Valley Tribal Park, Utah-Arizona.
Left, Buttes of the Cross, Canyonlands National Park, Utah.

Organ Mountains at sunset, New Mexico.

For the Knox, Harris, and McQuiston families
who came to the Southwest early on.

ACKNOWLEDGMENTS

To my father, for being there; to my wife, who
holds the keys; to Horton Grant, who has all the
answers; and to Joyce Sweet, who somehow got left
out last time.
                        —MICHAEL GRANT

I would like to thank my family—Marcy, Mikenna,
and Bryce—for their support and patience during
the production of this book. Also, many thanks to
the following: Heidi Redd and family of Dugout
Ranch, Utah; Ken and Jane Sleight and Pack
Creek Ranch, Utah; Bruce Hucko of Santa Fe,
New Mexico; Stan Dupuy of Bisbee, Arizona;
Teresa Cryns of Salt Lake City, Utah; Jay Saul of
Tucson, Arizona; and Jim and Peggy Nissen, Steve
and Vicki Mulligan, and Westlight Photography of
Moab, Utah. As always a special thanks to the
National Park Service, Forest Service, and BLM
for their support. The State Park systems of Utah,
Arizona, New Mexico, and Colorado were particu-
larity helpful and cooperative. I would also like to
thank Don McQuiston and Joyce Sweet for their
direction and encouragement.
                        —TOM TILL

Copyright © 1992 by Thunder Bay Press. All rights
reserved. No part of this book may be reproduced
in any form without written permission from the
publisher.

Library of Congress Cataloging-in-Publication Data
Grant, Michael, 1943–
    American Southwest: a land and its people/
written by Michael Grant: photography by
Tom Till.
        p.   cm.
    Includes bibliographical references.
    ISBN 0-934429-97-9: $50.00
    1. Southwest, New.   2. Southwest, New—
Pictorial works.   I. Till. Tom.   II. Title.
F787,G73   1992   879—dc20   92-8886 CIP
ISBN 0-934429-97-9
10 9 8 7 6 5 4 3 2 1

Printed in Hong Kong by Dai Nippon Printing
Co., Ltd.

Published by Thunder Bay Press
5880 Oberlin Drive
San Diego, CA 92121

Fresh snow at Betatakin Ruin, Navajo National Monument, Arizona.

INTRODUCTION

Not much is known, even in the New Mexico state archives, of the woman who first referred to the American Southwest as the Land of Enchantment. "It first showed up in a book by that title, by Lilian Whiting, in 1906," said New Mexico state historian Robert Torres. "She made it the title, and she also used it in the text. We don't know where she came from. The book was not a history, as such. It just described some of her travels in the area."

"The area" is a broad, rectangular section of the continent extending west from the 103rd to the 114th meridian, and north from the 32nd to the 38th parallel, a place of not only enchanting, but startling, beauty. It corresponds only roughly to political boundaries. The American Southwest, as described here, encompasses all of New Mexico and Arizona (still territories when Whiting was traveling there) and the southern quarters of Utah and Colorado, and its geology spills eastward into Texas as well, and south into Sonora and Chihuahua, Mexico.

Lilian Whiting may or may not have seen it all, but it was the New Mexico State Tourist Bureau that had the good sense, in 1935, to make a state slogan of "Land of Enchantment." In 1941 the slogan joined the sun symbol of the Zia Indian people on the state's auto license plates, and New Mexico has been the official Land of Enchantment since.

But a New Mexican, describing the Southwest for a visitor, could not stop with enchantment, though it is a fine place to start. By the time he was finished, he would realize that the Southwestern identity—more an aura, really—is a sum of contributions from its member states. From New Mexico comes enchantment, and distinctive Southwestern presences in art and architecture. Also, the Spaniards, in their explorations of the Southwest, arrived first in New Mexico and became the original ranchers there.

Colorado is a Spanish word for "red," the Southwestern landscape's predominant color. The original *colorado* reference, by Spanish explorers, was to the mighty river rushing down from the Rocky Mountains to cut unbelievable canyons in the great plateau. From Colorado the Southwest also gets its colorful reputation for grizzled prospectors combing rugged mountains, looking for—and finding—fabulous veins of silver and gold.

The visitor crossing into Arizona will notice that the state

Indian symbol above right; clouds, lightning and rain.

has two nicknames: "The Grand Canyon State" and "The Copper State." The Grand Canyon is to the Southwest as the Mona Lisa is to the Louvre—an international landmark for an otherwise fabulous collection. The copper lodes at Bisbee, Jerome, and Globe become true copies of fables from a land of unimaginable mineral wealth, where modern prospectors still die in attempts to find the legendary Lost Dutchman Mine. From Arizona come stories of one of the Southwest's most vivid figures—the cowboy, about whom stories are told that may be historic or imagined. Tourists in Paris, Frankfurt, and Tokyo are careful to include on their itineraries Tombstone, where Wyatt Earp and Doc Holliday faced off the Clanton brothers at the O.K. Corral. Arizona's cowboy reputation is well entrenched. If they thought they needed one, Arizonans could adopt a third nickname, "The Cowboy Movie Backdrop State."

From Utah, into the Southwest culture, came real cowboys and settlers, the Mormon farmers and ranchers arriving in wagon trains to build towns and settle the Arizona territory. Some of the Southwest's most spectacular geography—Zion National Park, Bryce Canyon, and Lake Powell—lies in Utah, and spectacular Monument Valley drops south from Utah into Arizona north of Kayenta. The name "Utah," incidentally, derives from the Navajo word for "upper," or "higher up," applied originally to Shoshone raiders, the "Utes," who came from the north to invade the Navajo lands.

The whole rich, deep Southwestern mystique is, of course, crowned by a headdress. Native American Indians were in residence in every part of the North American continent before Europeans knew the continent was here. Evidence of the Indians' legacy in the American experience begins at the Atlantic shore and stops at the Pacific. But the strongest association of Indians with New World America became an association with cowboys, a tableau peculiar to the West, and to the Southwest in particular.

The cowboy image has evolved into something modern and associated with helicopters. The Indian image has split into two, one of them a familiar stereotype conjuring visions of life on the old Southwest frontier. The other image is associated with a frontier, but not the old one. This is the image of the Indian as one who is descended from a living Earth, just as the mountains, the clouds, the trees, the rivers, the plants, and the animals are descended from that Earth, all existing in a state of balance and harmony. The Native American mythology, which Americans witness mostly through art and ritual, is directed toward maintaining that harmony. Not long ago, the industrialized society dismissed such ritual as "rain dances." Now that we find ourselves on a bleak, poisoned frontier where the trees are gone and the air is bad and the ozone has holes in it, a little Earth-human harmony is looking more and more like a good idea, or maybe a necessity.

Lilian Whiting might not have realized the kind of enchantment it is to stand in one place and see both the American future at perhaps its most imminent, and the American past certainly at its most recent. The Southwest was the last part of the continent to become one with the nation. Across the rest of the West, all the states had joined the Union by the turn of the century—California being the first, in 1850, and Utah the last, in 1896. Wyoming was admitted in 1890, Montana in 1889, and Colorado in 1876. New Mexico, the forty-seventh state, was admitted on January 6, 1912, and Arizona five weeks later, on February 14.

The feel of the old frontier lingers. Outside of their population centers, Arizona, New Mexico, and the southern tiers of Utah and Colorado have the lowest population per square mile in the United States. That kind of seclusion attracted scientists to Los Alamos, New Mexico, in the 1940s to assemble and test the first atomic bomb. The actual test took place far south of Los Alamos, at a site named Trinity, in the lava badlands of central New Mexico south of Bingham. The site today is closed to the public.

One reason for the low density in the Southwestern rural population is that the land and climate are harsh. A principal his-

12

torical contributor to the opening up of the American Southwest was the person who invented air conditioning. New Mexico, ranked fifth in area among all the states, has a population of only a little more than 1.5 million. Arizona, ranked sixth in area, has a population of more than 3.5 million, most of that concentrated in the Phoenix and Tucson metropolitan areas. Beyond the air conditioning, in any of the Southwest's quadrants, scenes of magnificent desolation wait for the next visitor to pass by. Tony Hillerman's novels are basically whodunits, mystery stories for which he has won national awards. But Hillerman is also a tour guide for the nation, describing in detail the beautiful lands at the conjunction of New Mexico, Arizona, and Utah. Humans can habitate these lands only by choice—the choice being to sacrifice creature comforts so that the soul may encounter glory. Such inhabitants bring an exclusivity to the land. The Navajo consider it holy. Visitors may get a glimpse, but nothing more, of the residing holiness, because they have not made the choice.

I was driving in that country—southwest from Ganado, where I had stopped at a trading post, Hubbell's, that has been doing business continually with the Navajo since 1880. The high plateau was essentially treeless, and dry, though that afternoon lacy showers of gray swept down from scattered clouds. It was beautiful country, and certainly qualifying as a place of magnificent desolation, but in driving through it, I had already begun to feel a strange sense of community. I wondered if it were the communion of humans with Earth, central to Navajo life. In the Navajo language, the people are Dineh, Earth is Dinetah. The highway, a good one, followed a long, shallow valley, and along the easy slope, below the ridgeline to the west, were occasional dwellings, well separated and well off the highway. It occurred to me that the Navajo liked things that way, not too close, space all around. It seemed to me that the Navajo Reservation had the continuity of a city, but a city flung over thousands of square miles, as if you had spread out each city block over one township (13,000 acres). This was community life arranged in balance with the earth. It explained, a few miles down the road, the existence of a sturdy, well-maintained sign in the middle of nowhere, advertising "Motorcycle Repair," with an arrow pointing down a straight, mile-long dirt road to a dwelling at the base of an ancient volcanic cone.

This was in the Castle Butte area, northeast of Winslow. The basic flat plane of the plateau was interrupted by lava cones and granite spires and looming buttes that looked like castles. The Painted Desert was nearby, and beyond it, in the western distance, stood the San Francisco Peaks, the highest in Arizona. The beauty here was improbable, and not far from Castle Butte stood a perfect demonstration of that implausibility.

Volcanic rock formations jutted straight up from the ground, 500 feet high, and they looked like long sheets of flame, captured in bronze by some supernatural sculptor, at the moment they vented from the earth. I could not imagine their creation in any but supernatural terms. I decided it would be fair to think of these bronze flames, and the spires and canyons and mountains and monuments of the Southwest as "supranatural," as in "above, beyond" what we might consider "ordinary" nature.

The supranatural earth events of long ago created three distinct land forms in the Southwest: mountains, a great plateau, and deserts. Utah, Arizona, and New Mexico all have mountain peaks higher than 12,000 feet. The southern terminus of the Rocky Mountains splits into three adjunct ranges in Colorado and northern New Mexico: the San Juan and Jemez mountains on the west and the Sangre de Cristo Mountains on the east. In between sit Santa Fe and the Rio Grande Valley. Wheeler Peak, New Mexico's highest (13,161 feet), is in the Sangre de Cristos, where author and poet D. H. Lawrence made his home and found his final resting place. The artist Georgia O'Keeffe made her home across the valley at Abiquiu, where the Chama River spills between the Jemez and San Juan ranges. Along the spines of the Jemez and (to

13

the north) the San Juans runs the Continental Divide. Drainage east of the Divide runs toward the Atlantic; drainage west runs to the Pacific. In the San Juans, which dominate southwestern Colorado, perch old Southwestern mining towns like Telluride, Silverton, Durango, and Creede. On the southwest slope of the San Juans, near the Four Corners area (where the four states—New Mexico, Colorado, Utah, and Arizona—meet at a single point) sits Mesa Verde, or "Green Mesa," with its pueblos that were a shining city in the Anasazi civilization a millenium ago.

On a simplified and foreshortened geological scale, the Rockies are new mountains. There were old, ancestor mountains in the West (which once was considerably east, on the shifting globe, of where it is now). The ancestor mountains eroded and washed down into great sedimentary seas. The sediments settled under the water and hardened (we are severely foreshortening now) into rock. In the meantime, the entire continental plate was floating west across the earth's subterranean, molten core. Eventually the continental plate came into contact with another plate that we now call the Pacific, a huge plate that wouldn't budge. The collision put what we now call the American West into considerable geological turmoil. Among other things, the Rockies were pushed up. The seas ran off. Through the cracked and crumbled crust rose fiery, volcanic energy, venting the eternal pressure of the earth's molten core. It was the same heat and pressure that drives the geysers today at Yellowstone, and vents itself occasionally at places like Mount Saint Helens, whose 1980 eruption was barely a hiccup on the scale under discussion. Hard rock mountains pushed up all over the Southwest. Vast blocks of earth rose and fell, tossed like petals on a stream. The old sedimentary seafloor was raised and bared to the sun and sky and wind. Lava fields the size of Delaware spread out across the plateau to cool like black, crystalline, supranatural fudge. Then came the glaciers.

When matters came to rest, they had left across the Southwest a topography shaped like stacked commas. The Rockies'

southwestern slopes nestle against the Colorado Plateau, which dominates southern Utah and arcs from northwest to southeast across northern and central Arizona toward New Mexico. On the plateau you can find rangeland, pastureland, conifer forests, canyon country, and high deserts. The Aquarius Plateau in south central Utah is, at 10,000 feet, the highest plane in the Colorado Plateau, and also the highest plateau in North America.

Not far south of Aquarius is Bryce Canyon, named for the Mormon settler Ebenezer Bryce, who ranched in the area until he wearied of losing cattle among the spectacular red chessmen standing in the canyon. Bryce is not a "canyon" at all, but the amazing erosive art of water, ice, and time on the soft face of the Pink Cliffs, part of a series of cliffs that steps south—The Grand Staircase, they call it—down to the Grand Canyon.

From the Grand Canyon, the plateau angles toward Flagstaff, following a curving escarpment called the Mogollon Rim toward the White Mountains, south of Springerville, and into New Mexico mesa country. The Colorado Plateau ends as you drive off the rim to the desert plains below, and the climate changes considerably. Along the Mogollon Rim spreads the largest stand of ponderosa pine in the world. Sixty-odd miles south is the desert metropolis of Phoenix, where summertime temperatures routinely top 110 degrees. From the Gulf of California, the Southwestern terrain within 250 miles passes through seven life zones to the Arctic-Tundra zone of Humphrey's Peak (12,663 feet) north of Flagstaff. The Southwest is North America's most varied region in geology, biology, and climatology. In the Southwest are more national parks (nine) and national park sites (forty-nine) than in any other region of the country.

The bottom comma of the Southwest is low-desert country, studded with volcanic, mineral-bearing mountains. Almost a million acres of low Arizona desert are irrigated and under cultivation, mostly around Phoenix and Yuma, yielding cotton—the state's number one crop—as well as produce and grains. This land

14

also supports a vital tourist crop, particularly in winter, when "snowbirds" line the parks with recreational vehicles carrying Canadian license plates. The desert west of Phoenix toward Wickenburg also hosts quite a few dude ranches and retirement homes.

From west to east, the Mojave, the Sonoran, and the Chihuahuan deserts dominate the landscape. At New Mexico's southeastern corner, the desert and mesa terrain give way to the perfectly flat Llano Estacado, which geographically merges the Southwest with the Texas Panhandle. The juxtaposition of Southwestern topography with the weather systems of the Great Plains gives New Mexico some of the most spectacular weather on earth.

Whatever the signals are that create the feeling in the brain which humans identify as "beauty," they were in place in the Southwest for millions of years before humans arrived. We now are certain that it is a compelling beauty, drawing people from around the world. It would be comforting to suppose that the first humans there, battling daily to survive, felt some compensatory glimmer of that same compulsion.

The newest archaeological evidence places humans in the Southwest at least thirty-five thousand years ago. That evidence, announced in early 1991, will require archaeologists to completely revise American prehistory. The objects recovered from a cave near Orogrande, New Mexico, included stone artifacts, hearths, a piece of a clay pot, and the bones of animals that researchers say were butchered. With that level of activity —"setting up house," so to speak—it becomes reasonable to suspect that humans were in the area for some significant period before the time indicated by carbon dating of the recently discovered artifacts. The general belief is that, whenever they arrived, the first people reached North America across a land bridge between Asia and Alaska.

Pueblo ruins, petroglyphs, and ancient kivas, or worship places, give obvious, and often stirring, evidence of more recent Southwestern civilizations. The people that the Navajos call Anasazi, or The Ancient Ones, are believed to have been inhabit-ing the Four Corners area at the time of Christ. The Southwestern Indian traditions of Earth mythology and ritual art trace back to the Anasazi, whose civilization flourished and then apparently was suddenly dispersed at the end of the thirteenth century—perhaps by marauders from the north, or by long and severe drought.

The Spanish were the first Europeans in the American Southwest, trekking up from Mexico City in the first half of the sixteenth century. They came looking for the legendary Seven Cities of Gold, or the Seven Cities of Cíbola, but found only Indian villages and spectacular scenery. The Spaniards established a province that they called New Mexico and put the capital at Santa Fe. With them they brought horses and sheep, the first providing previously unheard-of mobility to the Native Americans, and the latter providing a new industry that prevails to this day in tribal life. The Spanish also installed in the Southwest the second of the three cultural tiers that today define the Southwestern style.

Anglos arrived in the nineteenth century, lured initially by gold and silver, which they found. They too stayed to trade with the Indians, establish ranches, and live with the independence that was always plentiful on the frontier. In 1869 John Wesley Powell began his surveys of the Colorado and Green rivers and made the first call for water management, if the Southwest were to be settled. The Anglo westward migration was already at full stride, with the northern railroad reaching California in the 1860s, and the Santa Fe pushing through the Southwest in the 1880s. Access was all that was required for Anglos to discover the appeal of Southwestern beauty and culture. Entrepreneur Fred Harvey, working with the Atchison, Topeka, and Santa Fe Railway, recognized that appeal immediately in his plans to place comfortable hotels and restaurants along the route, and to provide markets for Indian crafts. By the turn of the century, Anglo settlers had added the third tier to the Southwestern style. Others came simply to feel the mystique and to enjoy the view; one of these was Lilian Whiting, and the "Land of Enchantment" was born. *Continued on page 20.*

15

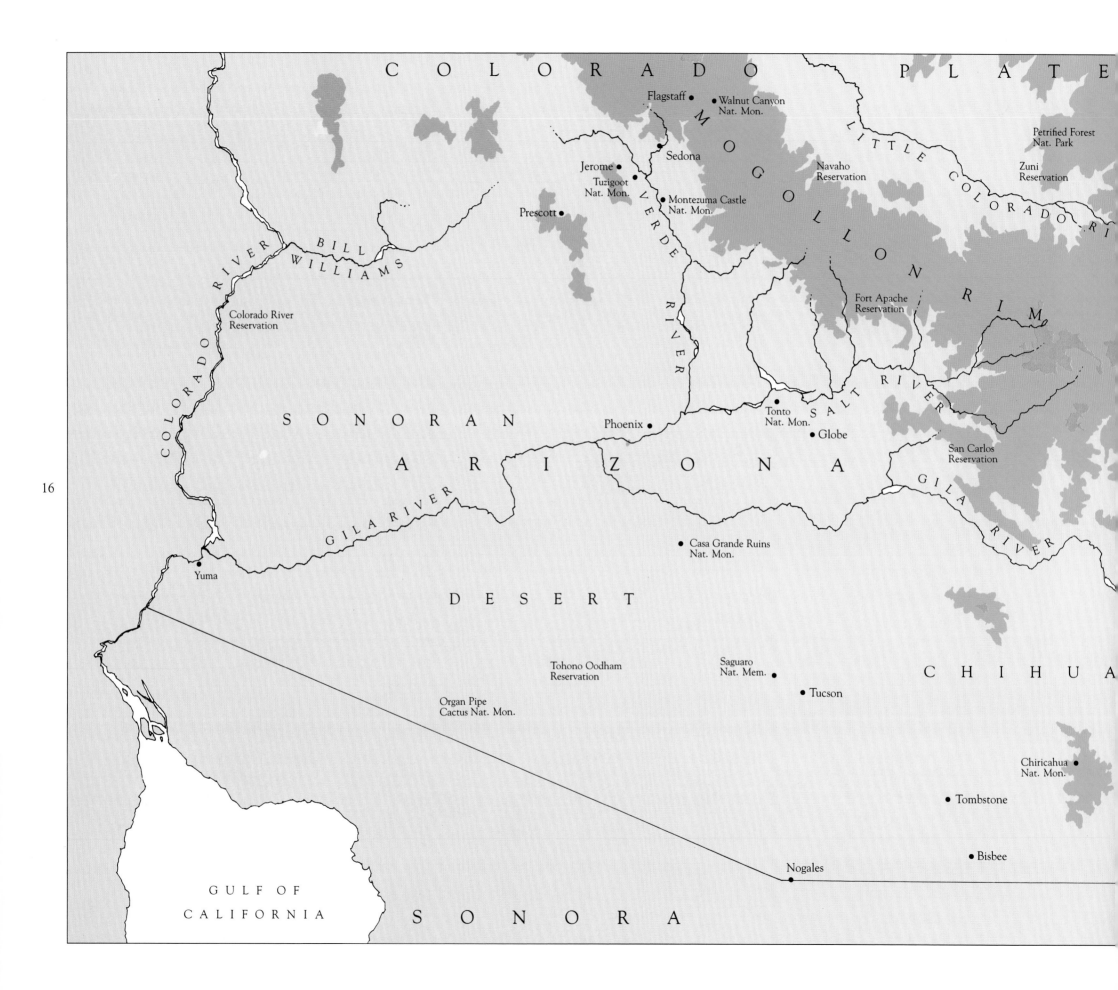

16

A   U

Zuni Pueblo

El Morro
Nat. Mon.

El Malpais
Nat. Mon.

Laguna Pueblo

Albuquerque

Ramah Navaho
Reservation

Canoncito
Reservation

Isleta Pueblo

Acoma
Pueblo

Isleta
Reservation

MANGAS
MTS.

DATIL MTS.

GALLINAS MTS.

Alamo Navaho
Reservation

Quarai at Salinas Pueblo
Missions Nat. Mon.

Grave of
Billy the Kid

Abo at Salinas Pueblo
Missions Nat. Mon.

Gran Quivera at Salinas
Pueblo Missions Nat. Mon.

PECOS RIVER

RIO GRANDE

MOGOLLON MTS.

MIMBRES MTS.

Gila Cliff
Dwellings
Nat. Mon.

N E W
M E X I C O

SAN ANDRES MTS.

Mescalero Apache
Reservation

GUADALUPE MTS.

17

Alamogordo

RIVER

White Sands
Nat. Mon.

HUAN

Las Cruces

Carlsbad Caverns
Nat. Park

D E S E R T

El Paso

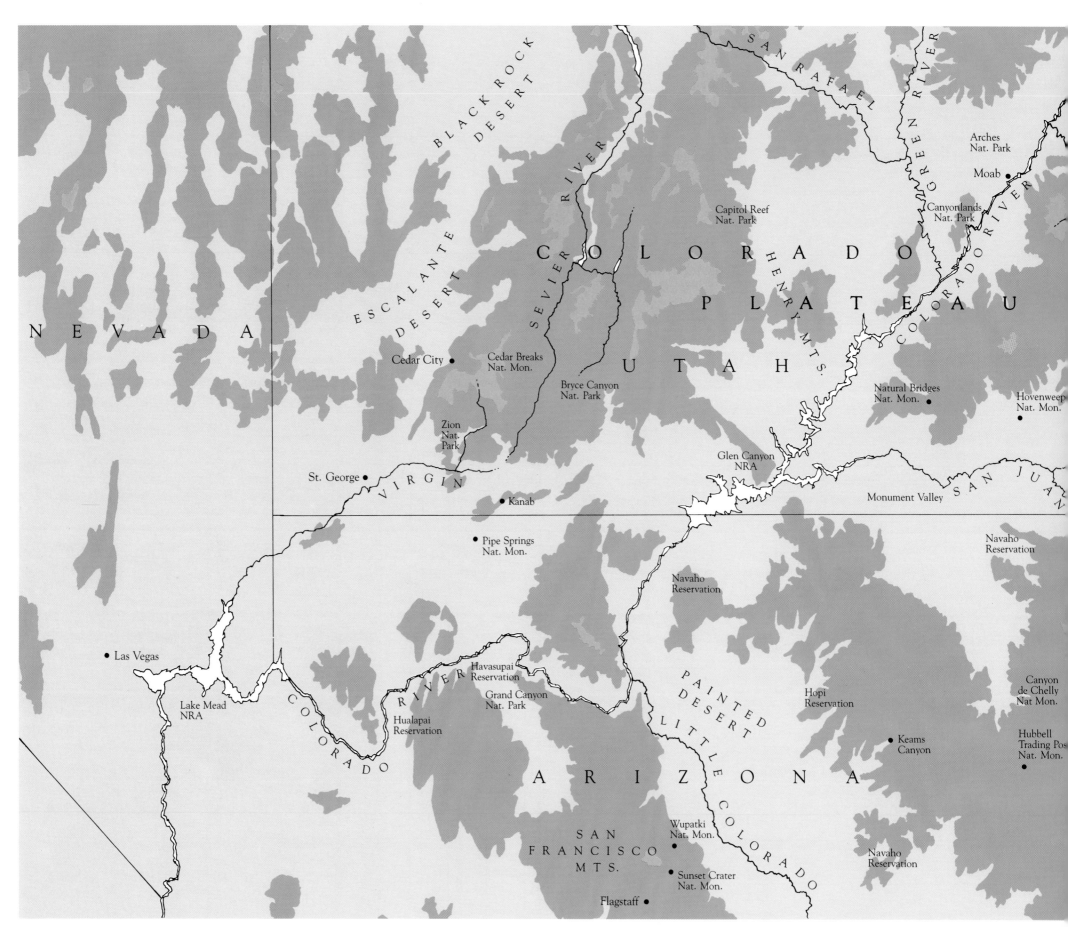

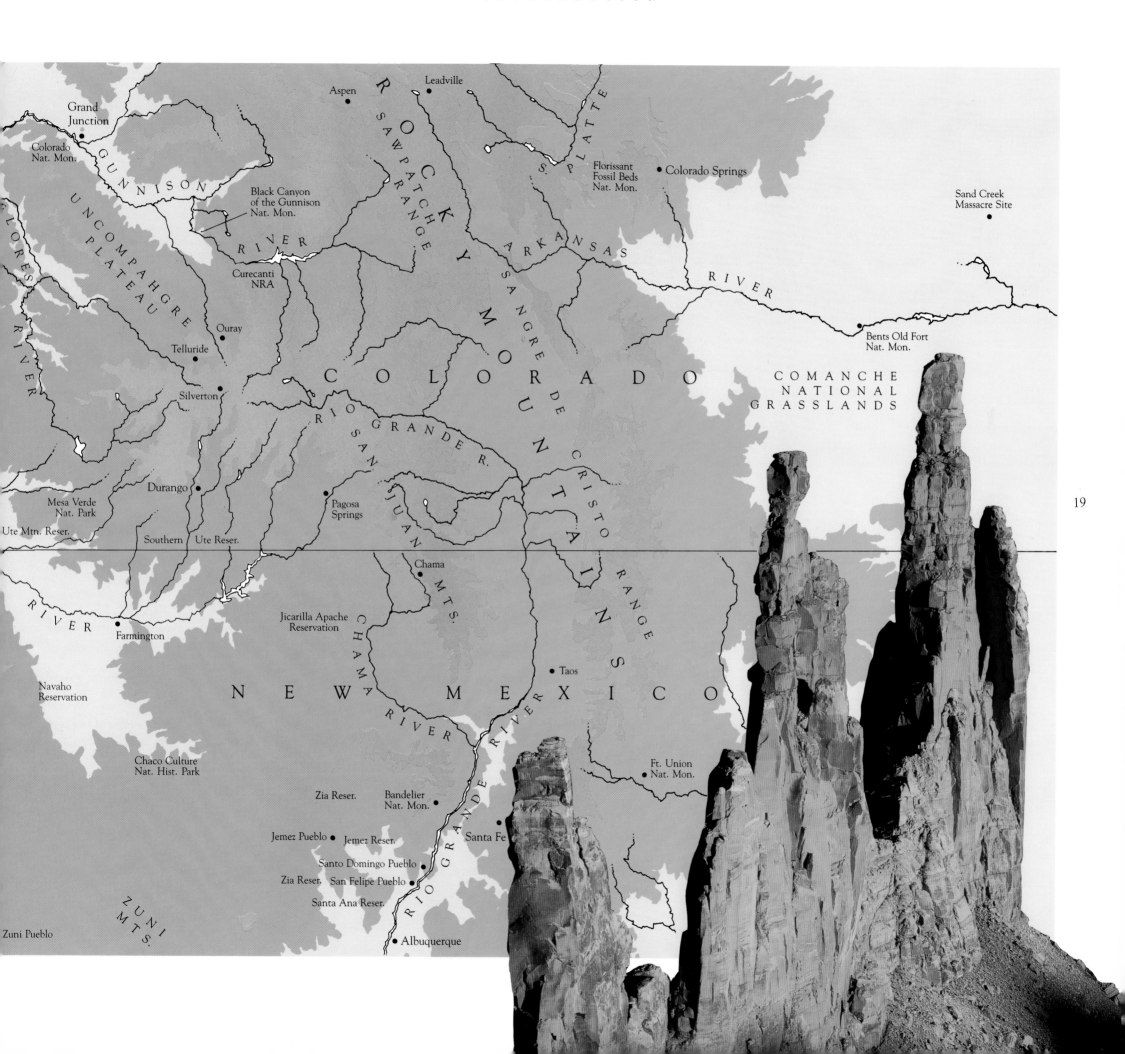

Among other things not known about Lilian Whiting is her possible relationship to the Whiting Brothers, whose long, yellow billboards became a Southwestern trademark after the 1930s. The national highway system was the last link in opening up the Southwest, and the famed U.S. Route 66 was America's "Main Street" to Santa Fe and Albuquerque and Gallup and Winslow and Flagstaff and the Grand Canyon. The Whiting Brothers, who started with a single station in St. Johns, Arizona, sold gasoline to these travelers, and advertised that fact with signs that stretched the length of a football field. I was among those travelers, in the days before Interstates, going with my family to Santa Fe and the Painted Desert and the Grand Canyon, and we would stay in places like Vaughn and Gallup, at motor courts named The Wagon Wheel, with gravel parking lots and big wagon-wheel signs lit up in neon against the red, dramatic sunsets.

Those days seem like the good old days. The Southwest, with the rest of the nation and the industrialized world, has hustled through the second half of the twentieth century toward the twenty-first. In the Southwest, perhaps more than anywhere, the sensation has been of moving along faster than people might like or think best. Limits suddenly started to be reached. Mineral resources played out, and mining towns became tourist towns. Growing cities put a strain on the Southwest's lifeline, the Colorado River. In 1991 a conservationist group named the Arizona stretch of the Colorado "America's most endangered river." State executives were considering "water summit" meetings, to revise or restrict water apportionments. Farmers blamed cities; cities blamed farmers. A national news magazine devoted a cover story to the problems of overuse of the West. Lined up on one side were economic interests, on the other, environmental interests. The basic question: How much civilization can the Southwest, whose appeal has always been greater than its resources, stand? Urbanite Southern Californians, fleeing a depressive economy, hooked up U-Hauls to their Wagoneers and started a movement some people called The Grapes of Math. Some of them went all the way back to Oklahoma, but most turned off in Flagstaff and Santa Fe, pumped California equity into expensive properties, placed added strains on utilities, and drove up the cost of living for everyone else. On its telephone tree, the Albuquerque Chamber of Commerce included an automatic extension for anyone considering a move there. In Santa Fe the Chamber began receiving three hundred queries a day. In the Southwest today, the fifth or sixth largest "population" in the region may be the number of motorists on Interstate 40 between Tucumcari and Kingman at any one time.

Among Southwesterners is a growing suspicion that harmony is out of balance in their own land, and restoration time is at hand. In Santa Fe, Albuquerque, and Phoenix newspapers on any given day, local and regional growth issues may dominate the front page. On one front page of the Santa Fe paper was a dispute over a gravel pit, a city council decision to buy land for affordable housing, and a suit to reverse a street extension project. In Tucson, an organization called the Southwest Public Recycling Association created a consortium of sixteen cities in Colorado, New Mexico, Nevada, Utah, Texas, and Arizona to pool materials for shipping to recyclers, making recycling programs more feasible for smaller cities. Organizers thought the consortium, by creating a dependable supply of material, might make the Southwest a major center for recycling. North of Tucson, meanwhile, private interests have built a huge greenhouse environment and named it Biosphere 2, the premise being that Earth is Biosphere 1. In the autumn of 1991, eight "Biospherians" were sealed into the environment, to live there for two years. Inside were replicas of an ocean, a savannah, and a rain forest; an area for growing crops; and four thousand varieties of animals and insects. A study of biospherian harmony was the Biospherians' stated goal, though some scientists didn't see much science present in the project, calling it Project Velcro.

Such future-think—however dubious, good, or proper—

comes very quickly upon a land whose past is so recent. On a summer evening my wife and I sat on the roof terrace at the old La Fonda Hotel in Santa Fe, bemused by the contradiction, across the street, of an antique Southwestern art gallery and a One-Hour Martinizing store side by side. It had not been so long ago that Mary Jane Coulter, who designed many of the Santa Fe buildings for Fred Harvey, was presiding over the design of La Fonda. I watched the sunset developing in brilliant reds and golds, framed beautifully through the dark, arched silhouette of La Fonda's bell tower. I sipped a margarita and imagined the year was 1950. Across the sunset, in the far, far distance, contrails appeared from two airliners, one eastbound, the other westbound. How accurate an image that would have been, I thought, for someone in 1950, trying to envision the Southwest's future from La Fonda's terrace.

Now that future is here; it has arrived with such swiftness in the Land of the Recent Past that poignant contrasts are made. On a rainy afternoon in Window Rock, governmental seat of the Navajo Nation, I stopped from curiosity to visit a huge, shiny supermarket, Basha's, on the town's west limits. It was as big and well-lit and attractively stocked a supermarket as I had ever seen in any city. I was walking back to the car when I heard an old, old voice, speaking in Navajo. I turned and saw an old woman, wrinkled and bent and wearing shapeless black and gray, speaking to a young, black-haired child who had moseyed from her side into the parking lot. Presumably she was calling him back to safety. Directly behind her loomed the soaring facade of Basha's. One of them was out of place.

Tularosa Basin, White Sands National Monument, New Mexico.

THE DESERTS

Sunset, Saguaro National Monument, Arizona.

TIME OF THE VISTAS

If you're not having a very good day, are convinced the world is against you, and feel like you could use some luck, consider this: by a grand design of incomprehensible scope, you and I and all the rest of the human beings in this part of the solar system are living at the exact right time—one lifetime out of 4.5 billion years—to best enjoy the beauty this planet has to offer.

Nowhere is that beauty more splendid than in the American Southwest. Airplanes—a new invention, developed in this century—can deliver you in hours from anywhere in the world to Phoenix or Albuquerque. In hours more, a rental car—faster, better engineered, and more luxurious than anything your grandfather could imagine—can deliver you to Oak Creek Canyon or Grand Canyon or Glen Canyon or Monument Valley or Zion or Bryce Canyon or the White Mountains or the Sangre de Cristos. The wide, smooth highways to these places have only been paved in the last fifty or sixty years.

Once you've arrived at the rim of Grand Canyon or the pueblos in Canyon de Chelly or Mesa Verde, you may linger for an hour or a day, and at night renew your strength in comfortable lodgings offering air conditioning, king-sized beds, cable television, and a variety of menu specialties prepared to perfection by expert chefs.

What you will see from the scenic overlooks are the remains of unimaginable events that occurred when the world was less hospitable than it has been lately. If even a pale imitation of such an event occurred today, we would call it grossly destructive, a terrible disaster. At the time, those events were definitely constructive. They built the Rocky Mountains and the Colorado Plateau.

It would have been something, to stand at a scenic overlook and watch the Rockies being built. But there were no roads then, no transportation, not much life, even. As they say, if earth's history were expressed in terms of one day, we humans would have shown up one second before midnight.

Time and scope don't permit a complete discussion of all that had to happen to produce the beauty of the American Southwest. Let's confine ourselves to more recent events. The North American continent had to pull away from Europe and drift into its present position north of the Tropic of Cancer. Some scrunching ensued. Subsurface Pacific and continental granite plates collided,

Indian symbol above right; Anasazi flute player petroglyph.

and where there had been a broad, flat, midcontinental sea, the Rocky Mountains were pushed up.

The planet was a lively place. Curious geologists—who must also feel they are living at exactly the right time—are discovering just how lively. Newspapers, magazines, and scientific journals are kept full of fascinating information about the birth and rebirth of life as the planet went through its creative throes. Evidence surfaced in 1991 suggesting that a huge volcanic eruption 250 million years ago, in what is now Siberia, may have caused the extinction of all life on the planet. It was a relatively short eruption—less than one million years, the geologists say—but it would have produced enough lava to cover the entire planet in a layer ten feet deep. These same geologists suggest that a later, minor eruption—lasting, say, 25,000 or 30,000 years—killed off the dinosaurs around 66 million years ago.

With such things going on, the world was definitely not ready for paved roads. At some point, 10 or 20 million years ago, the last plateau pushed upwards and settled back into place, the lurching and heaving stopped, the roaring subsided, and the planet came to rest. All that grandeur was in place, but still in the box, so to speak—ready for the wind and water to cut its final shape. A long wait began.

During the wait, the wind and the water did their work. The rivers—the Colorado, the Green, the San Juan, the Rio Grande—began their cuts down from the mountains through the raised sedimentary rock to the oceans. The weather and the ice ages rounded off the new edges, furrowed the raw slopes, and whisked away the loose earth between the towers, buttes, and mesas, eventually giving the land the shape we know today. For thousands or millions of years, the Southwest has appeared as it does now, with no one around to appreciate it. It is curiously wistful to think of Monument Valley on a summer day 50,000 years ago, washed by an afternoon thunderstorm, drenched by an evening sun, with not a soul to see.

Until recently, the archaeologists' best estimates put humans on the North American continent no more than 12,000 years ago. Then in 1991, inside a cave near Orogrande, New Mexico, forty miles east of Las Cruces, archaeologists found stone artifacts, bones from butchered animals, and hearths. A fragment of a clay pot seemed to carry on it the impression of a human fingerprint. Carbon dating established these fragments to be 35,000 years old. The first historically established Southwestern cultures, the Anasazi and Hohokam, would not appear in the area for another 33,000-plus years, until around the time of Christ. Anasazi living near Mesa Verde would have had to walk for weeks to get a glimpse of the Grand Canyon, if they were so inclined, and knew where to find it.

The first Europeans to reach the Southwest were Spanish explorers searching for the Seven Cities of Cíbola. They arrived around 450 years ago. We read their history and think of it as ancient. That history tells of Don Pedro de Tovar, a member of Coronado's expedition, being the first European to see the Grand Canyon, in 1540, coming upon it completely by accident.

By the early 1900s, the Santa Fe Railway had extensive trackage through the Southwest, including a spur to the Grand Canyon that cut the day-long stagecoach trip from Flagstaff to a comfortable train ride of three hours. From 1919 (the year it was made a national park) to 1929, the Grand Canyon's annual visitor count increased from 44,000 to 200,000.

There were not many roads yet. That demand was still to be created by developments in the automobile. A national highway act was signed into law in 1926. Not until 1938 was U.S. Route 66 completely paved from Chicago through Oklahoma, Texas, New Mexico, and Arizona, to California. Those arriving from the East on old Route 66, and later Interstate 40, found that the Southwest amazingly began on cue. The highway lies flat as a pancake across the Texas Panhandle. Almost simultaneous with its arrival at the border, the highway rolls off that table and drops down a little into

26

New Mexico country stamped with the red mesas, buttes, and arroyos that are the Southwest's signature.

The completion of Route 66 in the late 1930s marked the beginning of general access for tourists into the Southwest. That condition of general access is entering only its sixth decade. Already the original two-lane highways have been abandoned for wider, straighter, faster, multilane interstate successors. Paved feeder highways reach most of the remote corners. Jet travel places European visitors within a day and a night of the Southwestern vistas, and Asian visitors within two. Entire nations apparently pick up and make the trip. I stood on the Grand Canyon's packed South Rim one day, listened to the accent being spoken, and said, "If it's Tuesday, this must be Belgium." I was only half-kidding.

After these millions of years, with our luck to be born at this time of first access, the speed with which people come and go to places of such eternal beauty is utterly flabbergasting. They spend an hour at Grand Canyon, an hour at Zion, an hour at Bryce—less, if they are on a bus tour. I once drove straight through Monument Valley, traversing it in an hour en route to Lake Powell. Passing through Monument Valley to get to Lake Powell is like going through Heaven to get to Oz.

I did stop along the highway for a while, where the valley suddenly appears over a ridgeline north of Kayenta. Midday thundershowers were drifting across the land, and the beauty of it stopped me in my tracks. That visit was my first, and after the drive up U.S. 160 from Tuba City, I was puzzled by Kayenta. The whole route north from Flagstaff had been, well, spartan, with not much deference to tourists except for the gas stations and curio shops. Then here, in a pretty mountain setting, was a community, Kayenta, with amenities. Not only that, but amenities with connections to national chains: a couple of well-known motels; a couple of restaurants; a couple of fast-food places; somewhere—I didn't look, but I knew it was there—a vending box filled with copies of *USA Today*; neat grounds and paved, swept parking lots

to encourage tourists. Somebody knew something about Kayenta that I didn't.

When we departed the city on U.S. 163 to the north, I made the discovery. I knew from the map that Monument Valley was in the area, but I was not prepared to top a ridge and see it laid out beneath the scattered shadows of drifting rain showers. We stopped, took pictures, and pushed on to Lake Powell and a check-in time.

I think most people arrive at these vistas as I did—unprepared. They have made plans, but they are poor plans, calling for six vistas in a day with a check-in time at the end. Poor as the plans are, usually they are necessary, because there are only so many days in a week, so many weeks in a vacation.

The vistas, in the meantime, are numerous in this part of the world. Some of them are famous; some are historic; some are waiting for you, unmarked, not identified on the map, just around the next bend. Not much is made of the tourist attractiveness of the Mogollon Rim, for example, by those who have never made the drive south from Lake Mary through the Coconino National Forest through Strawberry and Payson down to Phoenix. That terrain reminds me of the Balcones Escarpment in Texas, where the Edwards Plateau drops down to the Coastal Plains—remarkable country, but no prettier even to Texas eyes than the descent off the Mogollon Rim below Strawberry.

In Arizona, between the highest point (Humphreys Peak, 12,670 feet) and the lowest (the Colorado River, 100 feet), all seven life zones are present. In New Mexico the biologists marvel at microclimates—complete, compact ecosystems created in unlikely places by combinations of weather and topography. Altitudes within the state range across two miles, from 13,160 feet at Wheeler Peak to 2,817 feet at the Red Bluff Reservoir. That range, juxtaposed with New Mexico's position on the flank of the Great Plains, where great storms gather, creates remarkable weather extremes. The difference between New Mexico's record high temperature (116 degrees at Artesia on June 29, 1918) and record low (minus 50 at Gavilan on February 1, 1951) is 166 degrees. Pajarito Canyon, in the Jemez Mountain range west of Albuquerque, ranks second in the nation, behind Tampa, Florida, for frequency of thunderstorms.

In no other part of the world are people so compelled out-of-doors. At Santa Fe, the opera house is open to the sky. Spectacular thunder and lightning accompanied the opening performance of the 1991 opera season (*La Traviata*), and nobody skipped a beat. The Southwest is a dynamic, beautiful land, rich with variations on its menu, a real three-course feast beneath the vertical, gravity-canceling Southwestern light. You can order from a number of mountain selections: the San Juans and Sangre de Cristos (the most beautiful he had ever seen, said author D. H. Lawrence) of Colorado and New Mexico; the San Francisco Peaks and White Mountains of Arizona; and the Cedar Breaks area around Brian Head in southwest Utah. The plateau country offers the Grand Canyon, which is a real wonder of the world and the Southwest's pièce de résistance, but also Lake Powell, Oak Creek Canyon, Jerome, the mesas of the Navajo and Hopi reservations, the Painted Desert, Monument Valley, the Anasazi pueblo country around the Four Corners, and the wonderful red mesas and reefs, particularly Enchanted Mesa, of western and central New Mexico. In the south lies the particular dignity of the Sonoran and Chihuahuan deserts, whose solitude and climate restore mind and body.

The American Automobile Association puts Arizona and New Mexico in the same tour book, and back-to-back on its highway map, treating them as an entry, acknowledging them as politi-

cal subdivisions of a deeper continuity: "the Great Southwest," C.B. deMille might say, "4.5 billion years in the making, the greatest spectacle on Earth."

I remember watching the television show "Jeopardy" one night, and the contestant in the middle was a man I'll call Bill. When the show's host, Alex Trebek, asked him what was interesting about his life, Bill said that every summer, for six weeks, he travels the Southwest by himself on a motorcycle. I couldn't say what that might imply in terms of Bill's personal or professional life, but in terms of seeing the Southwest, the man has a plan. Bill, a man of middle age, is particularly lucky to enjoy such a block of time. Usually, retired people are the ones criss-crossing the mountains, plateaus, and deserts for such extended periods. Each winter Arizona hosts a great many "snowbirds"—retired people who in October bring motor homes south from Canada, the Plains, and frigid Eastern points. From desert bases, they explore Southwestern vistas at their leisure until the following March. Some of them never go back north.

It was interesting that Bill told Alex Trebek he tours the Southwest for six weeks every summer. Obviously Bill reasons that he hasn't seen it all, or perhaps he simply hasn't seen enough of all of it. Nor have I, on either count. I don't have a motorcycle; I don't have six weeks off every summer; and I'm not ready to retire. But I do have a strategy: one vista per check-in time. I first thought of that strategy as I drove across Monument Valley in the rain that day, happy to learn about the motels in Kayenta. Call it a journey of discovery.

Monsoon storm clouds, Tuzigoot National Monument, north central Arizona.

29

Though the Southwest is portrayed as a land without rainfall, its sky is annually graced by summer clouds that ride monsoon wind currents up from the south, bearing not only moisture from the warm tropical seas, but also a beauty and an energy whose drama complements the events that shaped the land and the people who lived there. The Sinagua people who built these dwellings along the Verde River in Arizona understood the energy that the sky and the land possessed. Together, the sky and the land brought life. By them were the people sustained, and impressed with a humility that is probably the strongest and oldest characteristic of Southwestern civilization.

30

Snow on stone pinnacles, Chiricahua National Monument, southeastern Arizona.

Goodings verbena, near Bisbee, southeastern Arizona.

Arizona has its champions as the most beautiful of the fifty states, a beauty that comes in part from unpredictability. A visitor arriving in deepest southeastern Arizona with visions of desert-locked interstate highways in his mind may be astonished to find, in winter, snow-dusted volcanic rock pinnacles at the Chiricahua National Monument, which Arizonans call the Wonderland of Rocks. In spring, the brushy, semiarid landscape nearby will suddenly carpet itself in pink verbena.

32

Barrel cactus and boulders, Saguaro National Monument, Arizona.

The Southwest is a land where shape stands out. Out here, there is no missing the forest for the trees, or the stand for the yucca. Rugged individualism has always been the rule, both among the people and the plants that choose to put down roots here. Their character is plain to see, and often echoes the land's stark geometry. Southwestern shapes are all planes and angles; the pleated efficiency of the barrel cactus and the spiky resourcefulness of the yucca pick up the Southwestern light in precise patterns of light and shadow.

33

Yucca and ranchland, Lincoln National Forest, south central New Mexico.

34

God knew that Earth was going to be round and that the sun, to warm Earth sufficiently to abide life, would have to be hot. The trouble was, the heat could not fall uniformly on a round Earth. No matter how God oriented Earth, there would be a belt around it where the sun fell with more fury than God or man may have preferred. God could compensate by tipping the planet a little off a perpendicular axis—23.5 degrees, to be exact—so that the hot belt would slide up and down as Earth circled the sun, providing sunbelt people some relief for half the year. Still, in their summer half of the year, the light was so hot and bright at midday that God knew anything living in it was going to suffer. He thought such suffering deserved some immediate reward. So at the close of each day, through tricks of atmosphere and refraction, He turned the hard, bright light to softest gold. Anyone who has seen that light knows what a grand idea it was, and the people and things who live there fairly glow with gratitude.

Mission San Xavier del Bac, constructed 1783–1797, near Tucson, Arizona.

Sunset, Saguaro National Monument, Arizona.

36

Blooming aloe, Boyce Thompson Southwest Arboretum State Park, Arizona.

Barrel cactus with saguaros, Saguaro National Monument, Arizona.

Nature makes her own contracts. In some neighborhoods, credit is easy. The heavens regularly open up, and the rain comes down in buckets. The landscape is free to spend this largess in a few hundred different ways, producing grasses and hedges and floral and forest profusion on a Wagnerian scale. But in the Southwest, the heavens are stingier, and the contracts more delicately hammered out. The borrower, denied profusion, instead turns its efforts to brilliance. People who come to admire desert blooms like to wonder what colorful riots the aloe and cacti might produce, with decent rainfall. But of course in decent rainfall, the aloe and the cacti wouldn't grow.

38

Brittlebush and saguaros, Saguaro National Monument, Arizona.

Sunset, Organ Pipe Cactus National Monument, Arizona.

You could call the organ pipe cactus—as well as the saguaro—the sequoia of the desert, for making the most of what is available. Like the giant sequoias of California, the organ pipe tends to grow only in one place: desert acreage around the Ajo Mountains of southwestern Arizona that now has national monument status. While most desert growth tends to frugality of form, the cacti let it all hang out. Some saguaros grow to fifty feet and live for two hundred years. The organ pipe doesn't grow so tall because its stuffed-sock branching system occasionally appears to defy gravity.

Ranch barn, Capitol Reef National Park, Utah.

WORKING THE LAND

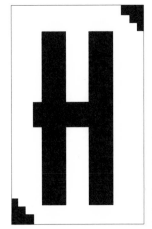

Harry Jones, seventy-odd years later, laughs when he remembers the day that Boog Burnett shot Jim Brown off his horse and killed him, on grazing land near Date Creek, Arizona. Harry was nearby, but he didn't see the event, or hear the rifle report, because he had just sliced off part of his own big toe.

Harry was about nine at the time. His dad, James Elias Jones, was one of several men who operated ranches in the Date Creek area, southwest of Prescott. Among these men, Jim Brown fell under suspicion of branding calves that did not belong to him.

"It was the Taylor grazing that caused it," said Harry Jones, who today, with Edna Mae, his wife of fifty-plus years, and his son Jim, ranches several thousand acres near Parker, Arizona.

"Taylor grazing" was sort of a collective grazing agreement authorized by Congress in the Taylor Act. This was in the 1920s. Then, as now, much of the Arizona landscape was controlled by the federal Bureau of Land Management, or BLM, which Jones and other Arizonans habitually call "the BL and M."

"This Taylor grazing was a federal act that set up grazing for ranchers, where they could graze on the BL and M land," said Harry. "Everyone just run their cattle together."

"They called it a grazing permit," said Edna Mae. "The Taylor Act gave the BL and M the authority to charge fees and set up designated areas for each rancher."

"But at the time of the Taylor grazing, there were no fences," said Harry.

"That's why the cattle got all mixed up," said Edna Mae. "And that's all that a roundup was. They gathered all the cattle, and each farmer and rancher would gather up his brand."

"It was kind of a mess," said Harry. "So this one ranch was having this roundup, and they accused Jim Brown of branding a calf that didn't belong to him. I guess they got into quite an argument about it."

Jones, as he told about this, sat with a white patch on his cheek, covering a place where the doctor had removed the kind of lesion caused by too much sun. He wore tan twill trousers, blue cotton short-sleeved shirt, string bola with a turquoise slide (Arizona's official neckwear), a straw rancher's hat, and dressy brown-and-tan boots. He wore wire-rim glasses, and his eyes were blue. He was born on September 16, 1915, on a ranch near Geronimo,

Indian symbol above right; clouds and rain.

Arizona, and hasn't much been off one since. He was a little embarrassed by the attention, and he didn't like tape recorders, but he was pleased to be talking about Arizona ranching, or "renching," as he pronounced it.

So this branding argument got under way one day among the cowboys. "The next day, why, they were coming up there in sight of Date Creek," said Harry, "and we were supposed to make lunch for them, my mother was, because that's where they were moving the cattle, moving them up there and working them.

"They were gonna come across the creek and eat, and then go back. We could hear them over there, with the cattle bawling and everything." At that moment Boog Burnett was riding toward Jim Brown with trouble on his mind.

Harry's mother said it was time to start warming everything up, that the cowboys would be coming across pretty soon. "So I went out to the woodpile and got a pan of chips and came back in, and instead of waiting for her—I wasn't very big—I took the lid off the stove, and I dropped it on my toe. Cut the end of my toe off. I was squalling so loud that we didn't hear the shot."

James Elias Jones reported later to his family that, as the men sat on their horses, Boog Burnett pulled his rifle out and said to Jim Brown, "I'm gonna kill you, you son of a bitch."

"And he did," said Harry. "Shot him off his horse. They just didn't like each other, and it rose from that, accusing each other of branding the wrong calves. Burnett turned around and rode off, and beat it to old Mexico. Stayed down there for years. He finally came back and went to trial, and he went to prison for a while."

Cowboy shoot-outs and cast-iron stove lids have pretty much passed from the Southwestern ranching tableau, and manufacturing and research have become the region's leading industries. But the livestock are still out there, and the cowboy still keeps his place as one of the Southwest's strongest mythic images. It was old-timer Van Holyoak, a Mormon rancher from around Showlow, who was selected to represent the whole state of Arizona at bicen-

tennial ceremonies in Washington, D.C., in 1976.

Arizona, despite drought in the late 1980s, counted 830,000 cattle and more than 250,000 sheep, while 1.7 million cattle and 578,000 sheep grazed New Mexico acreage. Ranching has been a principal Southwestern activity since the arrival of the Spanish, with their horses, in the sixteenth century. Livestock and minerals in abundance moved down the colonial highway from Santa Fe to Mexico City. Arizona still honors ranching as the state's oldest industry. By the mid-1800s, cattlemen were migrating from Texas and Utah to begin operations on the Colorado Plateau and in the Chihuahuan and Sonoran deserts.

Harry Jones's dad came to Arizona from Texas, by way of New Mexico. His mother came with her people down from Utah.

"The Mormons sent people out in every direction to start homes and towns," Harry said. "My mother's people left Pangwitch, Utah, in a wagon train, and came down and crossed the Colorado River at Lee's Ferry. They landed in Pima. My grandfather built the first house in Pima. Then they moved up around old Fort Thomas, started farming over there, and they put in an irrigation canal from the Gila River."

Not far away was the McEuen ranch, run by Felix and Sarah, who back in Texas, near Uvalde, had been neighbors to the Jones ranch. It was a hard life. Six months before James Elias Jones was born, his father died. Three days after he was born, his mother died. The McEuens took in the infant and "raised him up," as Harry Jones says, until he was four or five, when he went to live with an uncle in New Mexico. This was in the 1870s.

"His uncle was mean to him," said Harry, "so when he was twelve years old he decided to find out where the McEuens were. He found out they had left Texas and had a ranch in Arizona territory, about twenty miles west of Safford on the Gila River. He got on his horse one night and took out from New Mexico. He rode to Duncan, Arizona, real sick, and this fella took him in. My dad told him he was looking for the McEuen family that lived on the Gila

42

River someplace. This fella got ahold of the McEuens finally, and Mr. and Mrs. McEuen came up to Duncan in a wagon and picked him up and took him home. They kept him until he got married."

In those days Arizona was very much on the frontier, with nothing but ranching and farming, and a railway up to the mines around Globe. Harry grew up on horseback. "I remember riding in front on a saddle with my mother whenever we would go anyplace. We were going hunting one time, and they were talking as they were riding along. World War I had started, and they kept talking about this 'Kaiser'; they wished old 'Kaiser' would come out and they'd shoot him. And I thought it was a deer. I thought a deer was 'Kaiser' for the longest time.

"We lived right by the Apache Reservation. I was kinda raised up with the Indians. We got acquainted with a lot of them during the roundups. We'd have our roundups with some of the Indians coming with us, and when they had a roundup, why, we'd go over and ride with them."

This communal grazing, as with the Taylor Act to come, caused some mix-ups.

"The Indians would say the McEuens were stealing their cattle, and the McEuens would say the Indians were stealing our cattle. We went down to this little rodeo, and Mr. McEuen, he backed his horse in there, and went out to catch his calf, and he missed it. I was sitting by an old Indian on the fence there, and he said, 'Night no miss 'em.' I never forgot that."

Southwestern ranching falls into categories of rangeland grazing, on the plateau and in the mountain valleys; of grazing on irrigated pastureland below the plateau; and of desert "rustling," meaning that livestock rustle up the available desert feed. There is also the nomadic sheep ranching. Harry has had sheep, but didn't much like them.

"Cattle do better, in my opinion," he said. "The Basque mostly had the sheep. They came over here years ago, the sheep-herders, and got their own places. Back in the thirties, in the pretrucking days, they used the 'sheep trail.' It went from northeast of Phoenix to Showlow and northern Arizona. They would winter their sheep in the valley around Phoenix, then in the summer go back up north. This trail was five miles wide; they had a right-of-way through there."

Nowadays, of course, the 'sheep trail' is Interstate 17, and the herders hustle the sheep along in eighteen-wheelers. The developing twentith-century highway systems, said Harry Jones, have made Southwestern ranching, and agriculture in general, considerably more tolerable.

Less tolerable, sometimes, is the ranchers' traditional dependence on the BL and M for grazing land. That land is all fenced now, and the ranchers buy grazing permits, the BL and M charging them by the head.

"It's a big issue in Arizona," said Edna Mae Jones, a trim, amiable woman who gives the idea that, around the Joneses' Ganado Ranch, Harry herds the cattle and she herds the books. "We have a big argument about it every year. The BL and M wants to raise the permits so high that you can't afford to run any cattle."

"It was $1.85 a head, going up to $2-something," said Harry.

The Ganado Ranch is six townships—almost 140,000 acres—along the Colorado River near Parker. "It doesn't look like pastureland," said Edna Mae. "It looks like the low desert, which it is." In fact it is part of the Mojave Desert, which spills across the Colorado into western Arizona. The Ganado livestock are watered from six wells, ranging from three hundred to sixteen hundred feet deep, flowing at about twenty gallons per minute. Legally, the Joneses could send their livestock right down to the river to drink, and they used to do this, but now people mainly use the river for recreation.

Rainfall generates the feed. Not much rain falls on western and southwestern Arizona. A visitor would think nothing but cactus could survive there. But if you watch from an airliner at thirty-seven thousand feet, you will see, in the dun Arizona landscape,

43

signs of water everywhere. Rainfall follows squiggly lines from higher elevations to lower, where the lines spread out into washes and arroyos. They are almost always dry, but water has been there.

"There's more feed on that desert, you just don't know," said Edna Mae.

Rainy seasons come to Arizona in July and August, when tropical "monsoon" moisture moves north from Mexico, and in winter, when storms move down the Pacific Coast from the Gulf of Alaska.

"Any time it rains, and you get a quarter of an inch or more, you will get some feed, any time of the year," said Harry. "We have the galleta, sagebrush, Indian wheat, the brittlebush, six-weeks grass, the ironwood trees, the paloverde, the catclaw, and the mesquite. The six-weeks grass, if you get enough rain, comes up and gets about three to four inches high in about six weeks."

The Joneses run a Charolais-Brahma (they pronounce it "Braymer") mix, for a couple of reasons, one being the heat. "White" cattle stand the heat better than Herefords or, certainly, Black Angus. The other reason is foraging habits.

"The cattle have to roam and get the little clumps of feed. The whiteface and Angus, they're not as good at 'rustling' out on the range as your Braymer-and-Charolais cross," said Edna Mae.

"Any cross with a Braymer, they'll go out, say, eight miles from the water, where others will only go out five," said Harry. "We run right at six hundred mother cows, and you get an average of around seventy percent calf crop."

The result of this kind of grazing is a cow considered very attractive in the beef marketplace of the health-conscious 1990s. Consumers have begun to buy beef that is lower in fat and cholesterol content than the traditional, heavily marbled cuts obtained from feedlot cattle. One national beef wholesaler has begun marketing what it calls "SmartMeat," which is low-fat, low-cholesterol

44

beef from lean cattle, tenderized and injected with unsaturated vegetable oil to give it the marbled appearance. Food editors report these steaks cook up nice and tasty.

In his lifetime, Harry Jones has ranched in the mountains, in pastureland, and in the desert; all things considered, he says, he'll take the desert.

"It's about the same as on the plateau, you just have different types of weather and rainfall," he said. "If you get any moisture at all, why, I like the desert ranching as much as any other. Up there where you have the frost and ice, you have those seasons where nothing will grow. But down on the desert, like I say, any time you get rain—winter, summer, spring, or fall—why, you're gonna get some feed."

"As long as you get your feed, it's easier to control your cattle in the desert," said Edna Mae. "If you have your place up there in the forest, and get in where there's water and rain and feed everywhere, then when you gather your cattle, you've got to hard-cowboy them out of the forest area. In the desert, all you have to do is fence your waters. They all come in to water, and then all you have to do is close the gate."

Urban people have always thought of ranching as a romantic, but rough, way to make a living. They would picture it as hard, bare-knuckled work, even on lush pastureland ranches nearer the nation's "rain line"—the 100th meridian—where the grass is high and the water is deep. They would think of desert ranching in the deep Southwest as the activity of crazed hermits.

In reality, Harry and Edna Mae Jones preside over an Arizona desert spread where gentle rains bring year-round feed, grazed upon by self-herding cows that get sent off to a grateful market as the gourmet cattle of the new age. The beef is fine, but the irony is better.

Antique thresher, Pinos Altos ghost town, Gila National Forest, southwestern New Mexico.

45

When you park modern agricultural equipment next to earlier models, the invariable impression is that working the land must have been a real backbreaker. Iron wheels! Pulleys and belts! Mule teams! And the wooden equipment gives the impression of being heavy and rickety at the same time. Yet this old thresher made life easier in the wheat fields of old New Mexico. There is also a latent poetry of movement in the pulley wheels, and an element of art in the contrast of circles and squares, that is typical of nineteenth-century machinery.

46

Petroglyphs, Saguaro National Monument, Arizona.

Cowboys cooling off at a stock tank near Bingham, central New Mexico.

Modern Southwesterners enjoy many advantages over the ancient Southwesterners, among them an expanded knowledge of where, on the ground, they are. Not that the ancients were not curious. One day an ancient sat down to make a record of his travels. He thought about where he had been, and what he had seen. He had no idea of limitations of range, or of the existence of oceans, or of snowcaps or tropical rain forests. The world he knew was the world where his feet took him, and there was about that world a sameness. In that sameness, the ancient one found security. Wherever he moved, he was at the center of the world. His travels took him away from the center in the morning, and brought him back again at night. His idea of the world as a circle was, of course, a prescient view. And his urge to make a map presaged a modern desire, among dusty cowboys, to know where the stock tanks are.

48

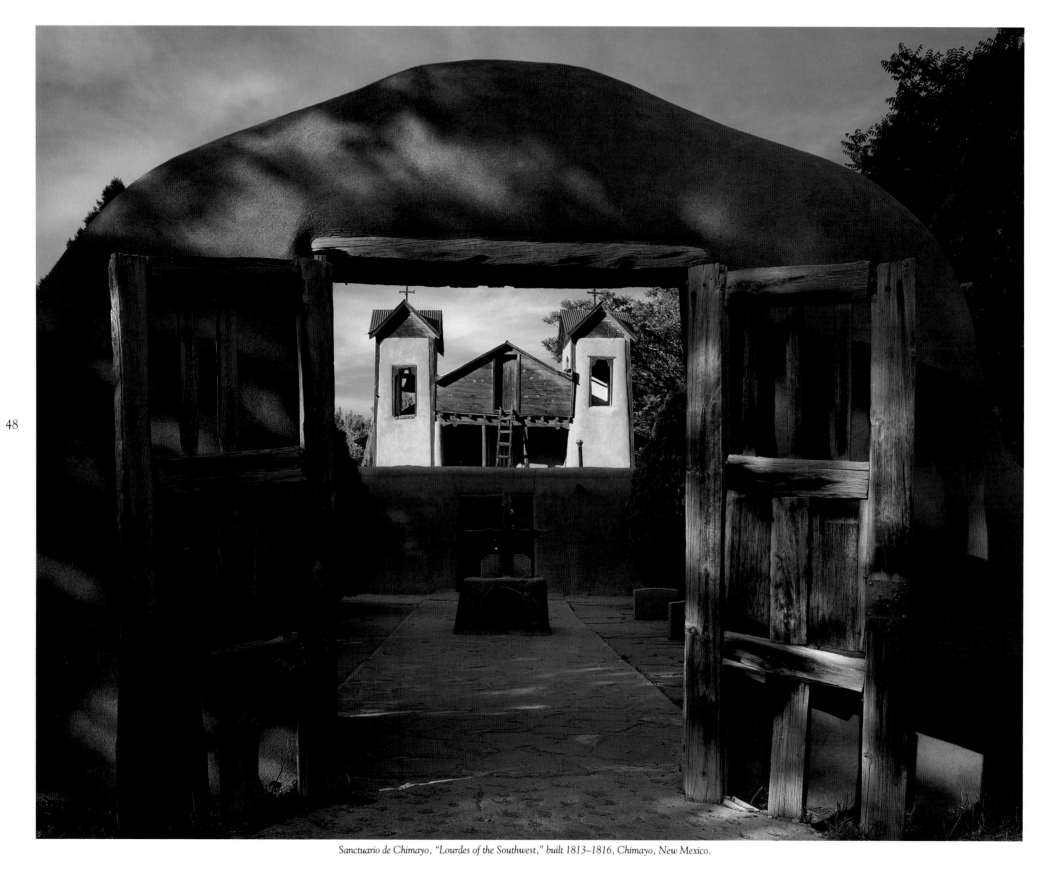

Sanctuario de Chimayo, "Lourdes of the Southwest," built 1813–1816, Chimayo, New Mexico.

Gran Quivera ruins, Salinas Pueblo Missions National Monument, central New Mexico.

The first generation of Southwesterners probably filtered down from the north, descendants of people who entered North America through Alaska, across a land bridge from Asia. From that seed the Anasazi culture rose, spreading out in latter-day tribes from the Four Corners area, leaving its mark in pueblos built of earth and stone. The second generation of Southwesterners arrived from the south, as Spanish civilization expanded out of Mexico in the sixteenth century. With them came Christianity and the Spanish rancho architecture that became modernized into the Santa Fe style.

Sometimes nature has disclosed her secrets without being asked, and sometimes humankind has helped her along. The white sands of south-central New Mexico originally were locked in gypsum deposits in the mountains. But the rains of the millenia washed the gypsum out of the mountains and onto the flats below. Time and wind evaporated the moisture and lifted the gypsum, swirling it into grains of sand, and shaping the sand into dunes whose splendor went virtually unnoticed for eons, until humankind tapped into nature's fossil-fuel secrets, with their applications for the wonders of internal combustion. This particular gas pump may have served scientists who first demonstrated, at the Trinity Site near here, what can happen when humankind succeeds in unlocking the secrets of the atom.

Deserted gas station, and sunrise over gypsum dunes, White Sands National Monument, New Mexico.

52

Sunset at petroglyphs site, Three Rivers National Recreation Area, New Mexico.

Flora and shrine, above Bisbee, Arizona.

Why would the hand in the petroglyph have six fingers, unless the artist did not create the hand in his own image, but in the image of someone greater than himself, whose work was so vast and mysterious that five fingers were not enough? From the beginning, the height and breadth of the Southwest has inspired its residents to reach for another, higher plane in seeking explanations for the grandeur of land and sky that in the same moment humbles the human presence, while giving flight to the human spirit. In this land, what couldn't be possible?

54

Poppies, Tonto National Monument, central Arizona

Overheard on a flight from San Diego to Atlanta:

"Mommy, what's that down there?"

"I think we must still be over Arizona."

"When does the ground get green again?"

"Not until Arkansas, honey."

"Does anybody live down there?"

"In Arizona? Sure. Lots of people live in Arizona."

"How can people live where there aren't any trees or grass?"

"Arizona has trees and grass. I think. Daddy and I drove through Arizona once, and I distinctly remember staying at a motel that had grass and trees."

"But how do they have grass and trees, when there isn't any water?"

"They have a little water."

"I don't see any. All I see is brown."

"Arizona is in the middle of a big desert, honey. They bring down their water in pipes, from Colorado."

"I think if I lived in Arizona, I would get sick of brown."

"It just all looks brown from way up here. If we were down there, you could see some grass and trees. Even flowers."

"Flowers? Down there?"

"Honey, I'm sure that, down there somewhere, you can find flowers in Arizona."

Spiderwort and cactus, Tonto National Monument, Arizona.

55

Front yard and old residence, Bisbee, Arizona.

CONSCIENCE & RESOURCES

They have their own municipal identities: Silverton, Bisbee, Jerome, Silver City, Creede, Morenci, and the others. And they have their individual personalities. But beneath all these Southwestern mining towns, there runs a vein of commonality. They are mountain towns. They were boom towns. They were, on the rugged frontier of the old Southwest, outposts of "civilized" culture, when mining moguls and managers brought with them such Eastern amenities as opera houses. They have become "scenic" towns. All the towns have rich stories to tell; to be such mean, dirty, common work, mining does inspire some of the most romantic history. And that history, after the mines gave out, became for these towns a major economic resource.

A few of the stories are widely familiar. Most people know about the legend of the Lost Dutchman gold mine, in the Superstition Mountains east of Phoenix.

Not as many people are aware that the fabled copper-mining town of Jerome was named for a New York banker who never visited there. Nor might they have heard of the prospector, down in Bisbee, who wagered his one-ninth interest in the Copper Queen mine against the notion that a horse could beat him in a footrace.

Too bad for those men. The one-ninth share turned out to be worth an estimated $40 million, and Jerome is a sight to see. No European alpine burg, no Tibetan mountain village, ever clung more precariously to its terrain than Jerome, perched on a thirty-degree slope two thousand feet above the Verde Valley. From the town's north city limit to the south limit, the elevation rises fifteen hundred feet. James S. Douglas built a mansion up there when he came to supervise the Little Daisy mine. Today the mansion houses the Jerome State Historic Park, and if you squint as you look northeast from the portico, you can read the names of the buildings in downtown Denver.

The towns are all more than a hundred years old, dating, like the stories, to the opening up of the Southwest's vast mineral resources in the second half of the nineteenth century. Gold and silver were the glamour lures, as always, but then, with developments in electricity and communications, a huge market opened up for copper. Most people know Arizona as the Grand Canyon State; its other nickname is the Copper State. The state's official neckwear—yes, the state of Arizona has an official neckwear—is a string bola tie, clasped with a silver and turquoise slide. Copper traces give turquoise its blue-green color.

The Bisbee prospector's name was George Warren. Of course there was not a "Bisbee" then, just the Rucker claim, filed in Tucson on August 6, 1877, by a couple of U.S. Army soldiers. Those soldiers, sent south out of Fort Bowie to scout for water, had found conspicuous deposits of copper ore in Mule Pass, through the Mule Mountains in southwestern Arizona. The soldiers' claim would become the fabled Copper Queen mine, or, as the locals called it, the Glory Hole.

The soldiers, their movements restricted by their assignments, hired George Warren to scout other claims. They might have hired a steadier hand. They grubstaked him with food, equipment, pack burros, and maybe some actual cash. Warren got drunk, sold the equipment, didn't follow through.

"It's hard to document George Warren," said Tom Vaughan, curator of the Bisbee Mining and Historical Museum. "No one knows exactly where he came from, back east or Montana, nobody knows. He was a prospector out here for years."

Warren remained in the area, naturally, there being a lot of copper and other minerals there. He staked several claims of his own in the late 1870s, and eventually he came into a one-ninth share of the mine that would become the Copper Queen. So the story goes. It may, said Tom Vaughan, be apocryphal.

"The story goes that Warren was in Charleston, which is a river town not far from here," said Vaughan. "He was in his cups one day in a saloon and got involved in a wager with the owner of the saloon, a Mr. Atkins. George said he could outrun Atkins's horse. The horse would have a rider. Warren and the horse would race fifty yards down to a stake and back. Warren's theory was that he could turn the stake faster than a horse could, that the horse would have to make a wide turn. He was accurate to a degree. He did do a good job down at the end of the stake; he was ahead of the horse at that point. But of course the straightaway was all

horse, and George lost his one-ninth interest in the mine."

The mine at that time was controlled by San Francisco interests, to whom the soldier-discoverers had sold out. Then in 1881, James A. Douglas, a Canadian by birth and a mining consultant, came from the East to represent Phelps-Dodge, a New York metals company, in Bisbee. On his recommendation, Phelps-Dodge bought the Atlanta mine, which was adjacent to the Copper Queen. Four years later, Phelps-Dodge bought the Copper Queen. Between 1885 and 1975, when Phelps-Dodge ceased its heavy mining operations in the area, Bisbee mines had produced metals—mainly copper, but also gold, silver, lead, and zinc—worth over $2 billion. For a little while, early in the twentieth century, Bisbee, population 25,000, was the largest city in Arizona.

The town of Douglas, twenty-five miles east of Bisbee, is named for James A. Douglas. Extracting copper from its ore required the use of huge, fire-powered smelters. Until 1900, Phelps-Dodge kept its smelting operation in Bisbee. But the narrow confines of Mule Pass restricted expansion and also affected the smelter's operation. "The smelter didn't draw well in the pass," said Tom Vaughan. "They had to have a flatter area where there was more room, and a good source of water, which they found over in that area to the east. The town that sprang up around the smelter was named Douglas."

James A. Douglas was known around Arizona as Dr. Douglas. "He didn't have a Ph.D.," said Tom Vaughan, "though he certainly had the intellect to hold a Ph.D., and he had many honorary university degrees. He not only had a great interest in geology and mining, but in many other subjects—natural history, current events. He never really lived in Bisbee, but he'd come here and lecture to the miners on diverse subjects. He would bring lantern slides from Japan, for example, or Egypt. He'd lecture on typhoid and how to avoid it. Dr. Douglas had a great interest in people as well as mining. We describe him often as a Renaissance man."

That would help explain the grandeur of the Douglas mansion and the Little Daisy Hotel in Jerome. The mansion, an Italianate villa perched on a promontory, was built by James S. Douglas, Dr. Douglas's son, after the younger Douglas bought the Little Daisy mine in 1910. The hotel, built to house the Little Daisy miners, looks—with its arched porticos—like a hotel you would build next to the Leaning Tower of Pisa. The hotel has stood vacant for decades, and no one has thought to tear it down.

Ironically, in 1880 Dr. Douglas had visited Cleopatra and Mingus mountains, where Jerome sits today, and saw copper ore, but not enough to overcome the problems of tough accessibility and inadequate transportation. He declined to invest. Other lease-holders persisted, including one who piqued the interest of a New York banker named Eugene Jerome. Mining, particularly smelting, was an expensive operation; equipment and fuel for the smelter had to be freighted by eighteen-horse wagon teams across hundreds of unpaved, sometimes unmarked, sometimes vertical miles. Jerome said he would underwrite the operation only if the mining camp were named for him.

The result was the United Verde Copper Company, which—under the ownership of the Clark family—would become the richest individually owned copper mine in the world.

James S. Douglas—his men called him Rawhide Jimmy, because of his tough work habits—came to Jerome after 1900 and in 1910 bought the Little Daisy mine, east of the United Verde operation. The Little Daisy was also across the Verde fault from the older, richer mine. Douglas and his geologists decided that the Verde fault, in some ancient slippage, had split the ore body, leaving part of it at the surface, where United Verde was operating, and carrying the other part deeper, where other geological activity covered it up. Douglas sent his Little Daisy miners down to find out. They struck one vein of ore that was an incredibly rich fifteen percent copper, and another vein that was forty-five percent.

These mineral riches did not come easily. The Southwest was a violent place. An hour's drive will take you down from Jerome,

across the Verde Valley floor, two thousand feet below, and up the valley's eastern wall, which is the Mogollon Rim, the boundary of the vast Colorado Plateau. No sooner are you on the plateau than you plunge into deep evergreen forests, an hour's drive and a world away from the harsh, desert, mineral-bearing mountains of Jerome.

Geologists say that the Southwest, along with most of the western part of the continent, once was flat and under water. When the seas receded, their floors hardened into sedimentary rock. All this while, the continental plate, having pulled away from what is now Europe, was drifting westward. When the continental plate ran into the Pacific plate, the result was like pushing a sheet of paper against a wall. The paper crumpled. Mountains— the Rockies and others—shot up, poking holes in the sedimentary sheet. Up with the mountains came the earth's bedrock, the extremely hard, dense rock that geologists call schist and gneiss, in whose fissures, for millions or billions of years, remained locked the pure mineral legacy—gold, silver, copper, lead, zinc—of the earth's molten origins.

There followed an era of intense volcanic activity, all over the West, as the crumpling paper relieved the molten pressure beneath the continental crust. That activity jumbled the incredible Southwestern landscape even more, creating the terrain over and around which prospectors—and before them, Native Americans— would creep and crawl, terrain in which a prospector could strike an incredible vein of gold, then turn around and never be able to find it again. Through that volcanic epoch, somehow, glided the great plateau, a huge sandstone ship riding out a molten hurricane. It is romantic today to stand on its western rail—the Mogollon Rim—and look across the deep to Jerome and the mountains jutted up, black granite whales breaching the desert sea.

In an incredibly brief period—barely a hundred years—the old mountains have been stripped of the treasures they clutched for so long. Technology, ever developing, now makes it profitable to extract copper from ore as sparse as one percent or less. Even

59

the tailings—the flat white acres of smelted earth that surround the old smelters—can be worked for their residual copper. Phelps-Dodge, maybe because it wanted to give something back, or maybe because it simply likes Arizona, moved its headquarters from New York to Phoenix in the 1980s. It maintains operations in the Southwest, but its big mining ventures, said Tom Vaughan, are overseas.

Jerome, Bisbee, Silverton, and the others have metamorphosed from mining centers to picturesque towns, places where wealth is no longer taken out, but carried in. For some reason, a reason as mysterious as the lure of gold for men, mining history is an incredibly rich romantic ore. Tourists no longer "bump into," as Tom Vaughan says, the old mining towns; the towns are placed on original itineraries, frequently by travel agencies, and often by travel agencies in Frankfurt and Tokyo. In the summer season the population of Silverton jumps by about five hundred every midday with the arrival from Durango of a steam-powered train. The Durango and Silverton Narrow Gauge Railroad uses tracks laid originally through the San Juan and La Plata mountains to move ore and equipment. Of course the ride is impossibly scenic.

Another tour-rail line, the Cumbres and Toltec Scenic Railroad, carries fifty thousand passengers a season on a 64-mile route, again on old mining track operated by the Denver and Rio Grande Western Railroad, from Antonito, Colorado, to Chama, New Mexico. The route, which zigzags back and forth across the Colorado–New Mexico border, climbs from 7,888 feet at Antonito through the San Juans to Cumbres Pass, at 10,015 feet, and glides down a four-percent grade to Chama. The train never reaches twenty miles per hour. The railhead at Antonito is 130 miles north of Santa Fe on scenic U.S. Highway 285, which passes right by Hernandez, New Mexico, where photographer Ansel Adams made his famous "Moonrise" portrait.

There has been talk about running a similar excursion train on old mining trackage between Bisbee and Tombstone, another old silver-mining town, whose mines played out before the turn of the century, but whose panache in the international tourist mind remains forever tied to Wyatt Earp and the O.K. Corral. Bisbee's jealousy of Tombstone's Hollywood reputation shows through when Bisbee people speak of the "facade" quality of Tombstone's buildings, as opposed to Bisbee's historic downtown, which survives more or less intact from early in the twentieth century.

"Bisbee suffered a series of fires and floods right at the turn of the century," said Stan Dupuy of the Chamber of Commerce. "Since there was so much money here, they rebuilt the town with brick, brought in on the railroad. They were able to hire some of the finest architects in the Southwest, and there was also the influence of the European miners. Bisbee has the flavor of a European town. Looking at it, you'd swear you were in Europe."

That could be one reason—but not the only reason, since it has happened in other mining towns—for the recent evolution in Bisbee of a thriving artists' colony. Bisbee has artists and brick, Tombstone has Wyatt Earp, Jerome has precipitous views, and Silverton has the railroad. All the towns still have their own identities, are still developing, and in some cases are still focused on going into a mountain. The last silver mine in Creede, Colorado (pop. 230), for example, closed in the 1980s, but only because silver prices fell so low. There is lots of silver left in the mines, where it will stay until the price comes to ten dollars or so. Creede families make a living in the tourist vein, operating galleries and shops and the Creede Repertory Theater. But they watch the paper for silver quotes and go to work feeling the pull of the mines.

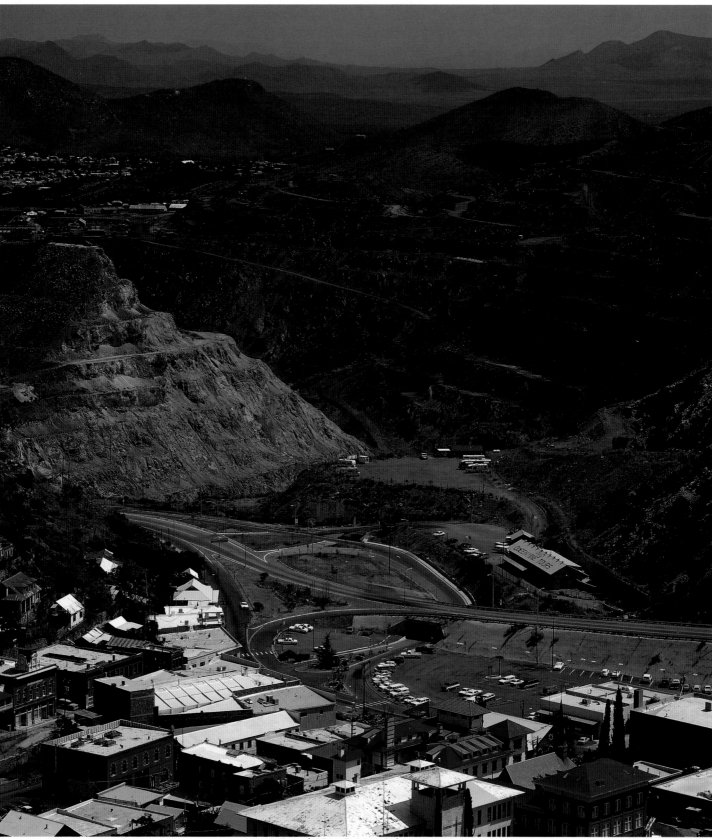

Lavender Open Pit Mine, Bisbee, Arizona.

As it happened, Arizona was green from the inside out. Native Americans worked the pretty green rock first, then in the late 1800s Europeans arrived and discovered ore as pure as forty-five percent copper, to feed into the nation's growing industrial engine. So abundant were the copper deposits buried in her soil that Arizona has two nicknames: The Grand Canyon State and The Copper State. Getting at the copper, at sites like Bisbee and Globe and Jerome, sometimes requires gouging distinctly unnatural contours into canyon profiles whose loss will always be felt, no matter how lightly they may have weighed against the gain.

The Lucky Cuss Bar, Tombstone, southeastern Arizona.

Locals at the bar, and Tombstone Epitaph *newspaper building, Tombstone, Arizona.*

Silver and gold brought the early prospectors to the site that Ed Schiefflin, the first and one of the most successful prospectors, named Tombstone. Underground water eventually closed the mines, but not before they produced millions of dollars' worth of ore, and seeded a legend that would produce millions more. The town's natural unruliness peaked in 1881 with a shoot-out between Wyatt Earp and the Clanton boys at the O.K. Corral. Early in the twentieth century, silver reentered the town's picture in the form of the silver nitrate component of movie film. The name Tombstone became symbolic of the Old West cowboy town. Travel agents around the world routinely include Tombstone on their Southwestern tour bus itineraries. It irks some folks in Bisbee, which has a colorful history of its own, that the tourists come down old U.S. 80 only as far as Tombstone, then turn back to Tucson, figuring they've seen it all.

64

Blooming datura and Mule Mountains, Jerome, north central Arizona.

Leo T. Picone of Superior, Arizona, and Coke sign, Jerome, Arizona.

Mineral recovery still goes on in the Arizona mining towns, but not on the grand scale of the old days. Secondary extraction technology has replaced primary extraction, whose heyday was mostly past by the mid-twentieth century. Toward the end of that century, the towns started to change directions. Like old Coca-Cola signs, as their original purpose faded, they started to take on the rustic patina of history, which inspires its own affection. For many, the mining towns still present a living history, wherever old-timers gather at familiar conversation spots to sit and pass some time and talk things over.

66

Pinos Altos Opera House, Pinos Altos ghost town, New Mexico.

The Southwest had its cowboys and miners and mountain men, but the urban society arriving from the East also brought "civilization," as it manifests itself in culture and fine things. Fred Harvey and the Harvey Girls, following the progress of the Santa Fe Railway across the Southwest, established restaurants and hotels that operated on strict principles of civility, crisp aprons, and white linen. Though the frontier towns found such culture a bit starchy, sooner or later they came to emulate that civility, because it was lawful and reassuring. Harvey has been described as the first civilizing force in the Southwest. The new railroads, meanwhile, brought performers and singers and acting troupes to fill the opera houses, as well as clothing, cloth, fragrances, medications, and tools to fill the frontier merchants' shelves.

Zearing's Mercantile Building, Benson, southeastern Arizona.

68

Carlsbad County Courthouse, Carlsbad, southeastern New Mexico.

Antique signs, Cibola National Forest, west central New Mexico.

Catchy slogans, posted along the highways, were nothing new in a country where landowners for generations had been pouring pride and ego into clever symbols to identify their property. Madison Avenue imagemakers might have had the good idea—it would still be a good idea today—to retain a Southwestern rancher as a creative consultant. Nowhere will be found a breed of people more devoted to the cause of identity, or to expressing it effectively. And as you can tell from the portal at the Carlsbad County Courthouse, the competition to be creative was fierce.

Winter sunrise, Monument Valley, Arizona.

THE PLATEAU

Evening clouds, Mather Point, South Rim, Grand Canyon National Park, Arizona.

THE GRAND CANYON

They may not have had names, but they had identities. Family members were known to each other, and to members of other families in the group. Among these families traveling together, a hierarchy would have emerged. There would have been a leader. They were relative newcomers on the planet, though after a million years of walking plateaus such as this, certain survival senses—some based in instinct, others acquired—would have evolved.

It was such a sense—a sense of something being out there—that caused the leader to stop in midstride. The night was dark, moonless. How did they think of the moon? What did they call it? They would have thought the moon was good, because it gave them vision, like the sun. In a certain rhythm it returned to reward them with a faint extension of the day. The leader knew what this rhythm was. The knowledge was one of the things that made him leader. He knew the pale light would come tonight, but they could not wait for it. The air was cool, but the leader could feel colder wind coming, hear it in the tops of the trees, and the group had not yet found shelter.

The people had come from the north—foraging, hunting, surviving. They carried within themselves the genetic heritage of generations that long ago had crossed a frozen land bridge, searching for a route to the sun, which lay low and cold in the southern sky and sometimes did not appear at all.

The leader knew without knowing that his direction carried the group still nearer the sun, whose warmth provided his people a primitive, fundamental freedom. When the sun left, it took with it that freedom. The night also took their vision and gave it to their predators. The night was a time of need, a blind harbinger of fear, the crucible of faith.

Now the group had emerged from the thin forest, and the leader stopped suddenly in his tracks. He stared into the blackness, straining to see the thing that he could feel. He took another tentative step and was flooded with fear of an intensity that bumped him backward and shook him like wind shook the leaves. He did not know what was there, but he knew he could not meet it without vision. He turned the group back toward the trees, where eventually they slept.

Later in the night the moonlight came—pale, illuminating

73

Indian symbol above right; bird.

fingers creeping from the east, fanning out over the great plateau toward the opposite horizon. The light reached the place where lay the group from the north. It spread across the flat, hard ground beyond the trees like pearly water rising. Suddenly something stopped the light's advance. At a point along a line paralleling the forest, the light seemed simply to disappear, like water over a falls. Beyond that line the earth, under the rising moon, remained as black as the sky.

The leader stepped into the light and peered across the pearly median at the earth that swallowed moonlight. He wondered: Will this strange, black earth swallow the light that gives us vision as well? He felt great fear, but also the strange, instinctive elation of a journey completed, a purpose fulfilled, a primeval sense of going full circle. They had come in search of the sun and had arrived at a place where, perhaps, the sun ended.

The others in the group cowered like animals, but the leader, as if magnetized, continued to watch, and as he did he saw the pearly light rise again at a great distance across the void. A mountain grew from the blackness, a mountain with steep sides that rested on nothing. A second mountain appeared, and a third, and then more, until the void became filled with beautiful, floating mountains.

The leader thought it must be another of those strange dances created by his brother who lived in the earth. That brother followed him wherever he went, moved exactly as he moved, sat when he sat, ran when he ran. The earth brother was always there, a living part of the leader, as much a part of him as his own arm. Only when the leader leaped, as if from boulder to boulder, were he and his earth brother separated, but then his earth brother pulled him immediately back.

The leader accepted the reality that he and his earth brother shared a common soul. His belief was genuine, that he and the earth were one. Further, all the animals, the trees, the rocks, the mountains, even the clouds, had earth souls. All things, the

leader saw, were born of the earth spirit, to which all things returned, even the birds. The hawk and the eagle, though they might soar for hours, eventually would be pulled to earth by their earth brothers.

The leader could get closest to his earth brother by huddling near him. Every night when he slept, he returned to the realm of the earth brother. It was in that realm that the earth brother created his strange dances, few of which the leader had ever seen in the Vision World. The figures in the dances were always larger, sometimes vastly so, than he. He accepted their size as natural, because they were creatures that dwelled in the earth's vast realm. Nevertheless, they frightened him so much that sometimes he carried their memory into the Vision World.

Now, watching the beautiful, floating mountains, the leader believed he must be seeing another of the strange dances. But those spirits had visited him only behind closed eyes. He closed his eyes, and the floating mountains disappeared. He opened his eyes, and the mountains reappeared. He stood that way, fearful of turning his back on the earth spirits, until the light that brought vision came.

In the history of humankind, moments have arrived with information that, in the space of an instant, or an hour, forever changed the human mind. This imaginary dawn on the plateau might have brought such a moment. The light of dawn warmed the black of night; black melted into gray and seeped back into the earth, revealing the earth's form—a form that provided the leader not relief from dreams, but new, entirely original circumstances that in moments canceled every physical and spiritual bargain he had managed to make with the Vision World.

What had stopped him like a wall in the night was the rim of a canyon. Over the rim was a vertical drop of several hundred feet. From the rim, he and his group were looking across a canyon ten miles wide and more than a mile deep. But he and his people did not enjoy the reassurance of numbers. They lacked any means at all to gauge the canyon, to restrict it, to bring it under control. The canyon boomed in their minds, blowing away at a glance whatever sense of proportion they had managed to develop over a million years.

They would have preferred to flee such devastation, but it was too late. They had seen, and now they had no choice. From that moment, humans in the southwestern part of this continent began to rebuild their place in the world on a completely different scale. Their reverence for the earth thereafter would have no human measure.

In another few tens of thousands of years, after the Sumerians had devised a means of writing, and the Phoenicians had given the Western world its alphabet, the word *quintessence*—from the Latin term for "the fifth essence"—came to mean "without peer," or "the sum of all others." Eventually the Europeans, not satisfied with the ring of "quintessent opera," would supply a synonym, "grand." Thus the Spaniards, arriving at the rim around 1540, would have known it was the earth's quintessential canyon, but they called it grand.

The first people ever to reach the rim—the leader and his group—had in fact come full circle. On the rim, they stood as the record of humankind to that point. Before and below them lay the record, to that point, of the earth that bore them. Had he known about physics and big bangs and coalescence of cosmic clouds into solar systems, the leader might have descended to the canyon's floor and found rock laid down hundreds of millions of years before the original carbon-oxygen cellular intercourse upon which his life would eventually hinge.

Of course that would be the modern, scientific view. But the leader's view, primitive and mystic, might have been much the same. Here, he might have decided—with as much awe as the geologists coming later would feel—is where the world began. If there were a center from which all things sprang, this opening most certainly would lead to it. From down there came the earth,

the sun, the moon, the mountains, the clouds, the rivers, the trees, the animals, and the people. Now the people had found their way back again. Here was a sacred place.

The people knew that. Their only sacrament was fear, and here was the most fearful of places, the giver—and perhaps taker—of all life. They saw the canyon as alive and sought to appease it. Their actions on the rim at that first sunrise might have expressed the same sort of direction that the post-Phoenicians came to classify as homage to a person held in reverence.

But what sort of person? What manner of earth brother must live in that place: a brother who walks at the center of the world and devours light and throws up floating mountains in the night? His would have been a power not of the known earth, even within, or beyond, the dream realm. At the rim that morning there might have occurred one of humankind's first encounters with the concept now defined as "god: any of various beings conceived of as supernatural, immortal, and having special powers over people and nature." From the first moment, the canyon took its place in the human experience as compelling evidence for a spiritual presence in the physical world. People still go there to pay homage.

The first people at the rim, with no mental control over the canyon's size, or familiarity with the spirits that dwelled there (or even a clear idea of what a spirit was), would not have entered the canyon at all. The canyon became the constant enterer, into the consciousness of anyone who looked on it. Smaller, more manageable canyons became—and remain—sacred sites in ancient native Southwestern rituals. They were the rituals of origins, of where the people came from.

But around the Grand Canyon, for many thousands of years—most of an epoch—people continued to circle, held back by sheer geographical intimidation and the other, deeper doubts that go with disturbing the silences one finds toward the bottom of a canyon that is a mile deep.

75

What became of the first people at the rim, no one can say. The leader, wanting to find a way around it, may have turned east, pretty soon finding that the canyon rim took him north again, away from the sun. Had he turned west—following the sun, so to speak—he and his group might have found the broad canyon that eventually would become the home of the Havasupai, a tribe that was established in the canyon by the time the Spanish explorers arrived in the sixteenth century.

The only route around the canyon available to groups today takes the eastern loop. The loop traverses a distance of 214 miles from the North Rim to the South Rim. The driving time is between five and six hours. If a western loop were ever built, people could drive completely around the Grand Canyon in about the same time they could drive from Flagstaff, Arizona, to Tucumcari, New Mexico.

Humans, but not many, today regularly descend into the canyon, all the way to the floor and the Colorado River. The guidebooks describe the trips, on muleback, as "strenuous," to be undertaken "only by those in good physical condition." Further, for safety purposes, people making the trip must be "English-speaking persons [excluding a large percentage of all canyon visitors today] measuring over 4 feet 7 inches tall and weighing under 200 pounds when fully dressed [excluding another considerable percentage]." Thus maybe only one percent of all visitors have actually descended into the canyon.

Hikers may also cross from the South Rim to the North Rim. This trip is recommended only for "hardy" individuals. From the first visitors in antiquity to those arriving tomorrow, only the hardiest have reached the canyon depths. No record of such a descent existed at all by the time of John Wesley Powell's 1869 river expedition through the canyon.

But all visitors, from the first to the last to the most Belgian to the most rotund, share the common destination. All who arrive at the canyon rim have come full circle: they represent the record of civilization to this point; the canyon reveals the record of the earth that bore them. And all carry images away with them from the canyon. No one has made a study, as has been made of famous faces, but if you asked which photo or snapshot of a place appears in more homes worldwide than any other, it might be of the Grand Canyon.

The primitive leader and his people carried their own image away, an image that was passed on as the people, having encountered the canyon, sought to rebuild their world on that completely new scale.

In the Southwest, and through Central America onto the South American plains, people of antiquity have left distinctive marks from their civilizations. Some of these are giant shapes—earth reliefs—stamped into the ground. Only from airplane altitudes do the reliefs become visible as the shapes of giant animals and human beings. Several theories have been devised to explain the existence of these shapes, including the notion that, since they take shape only from above, they must have been put there at the direction of flying-saucer-equipped visitors from space.

There is another theory, certainly romantic, probably original with these pages. But the giant figures in the deserts and plains may have been placed there as shadows—earth brothers of a people striving to cast human shadows on the scale they found at the great canyon on the high Southwestern plateau.

Colorado River, in the western Grand Canyon, from the South Rim.

You can think of the Grand Canyon as a monument to a river. It was the mighty Colorado River, gathering in the Rocky Mountains and thundering down and across the great plateau, that sustained life in the Southwest since the earliest days of habitation by men or beasts. En route, the river cut through the old, sedimentary seabeds, deeper and nearer to the earth's earliest geology. By the 1990s, the river, dammed and drained and overextended, was only an echo of the original. But the canyon tells all who come, "A mighty river passed this way."

78

Storm clouds, Colorado National Monument, Colorado.

Rainbow over the Canyonlands at sunset, Dead Horse Point State Park, Utah.

Physicists now can tell us how it works—the remarkable design of frequencies and wavelengths arranged across a spectrum, creating colors that interact in various ways. Red, for example, reinforces blue; and blue, the physicists explain, reinforces red. Anyone who ever visited the Southwest would wonder where the physicists had been, all these years. What they haven't explained yet is the effect on the spirit of the mutual red-blue reinforcement in the presence of storm clouds and horizontal light.

80

Dawn, Mesa Arch, Canyonlands National Park, Utah.

Cores boiled. Crusts cooled. Volcanos spewed. Plates formed and shifted. Mountains were thrust up. The elements wore the mountains down to plains. Seas covered the plains, but parted when continental plates met and cracked the plains and shoved up old rock from deep below. Ice came and went, volcanos returned, the plateaus rose and fell with the heaving of the mountains. The results were not homogenous. If the Southwest were ice cream, it would be Rocky Road. In the prehistoric mixing bowl, nature's spatula swirled hard rock through softer rock. When the rock cooled, and the wind and the water went to work, the soft rock dissolved first, revealing the incredible loops and sworls and spires of the harder rock that had been stirred in so long ago. The formations are breathtaking—photographers owe a huge debt to the Precambrian Period— but, admiring them, you have to wonder how more breathtaking was their creation.

81

North Mitten spire, Monument Valley, Utah-Arizona.

82

El Morro Spring, El Morro National Monument, New Mexico.

In their own minds, humans are bigger than they really are. Such an overestimation comes with knowledge. As humans have accumulated knowledge about their planet, they have decided that, in the overall scale of things, they are about the right size. They have seen photos from outer space that shrink the globe to a big blue marble. In fact, with the new whiz-bang perspectives, people cast off humility and common sense, and make the mistake of thinking they may be bigger than the planet. The Native American who lived in this land had no such problem. His only idea of scale was provided by the landscape around and over him, in which he stood properly small. That scale remains unchanged throughout the Southwest, deflating the self-images of any globe-trotters who visit there and stand before the glory of human scale in its original design, a perspective that was meant to be, and that will endure.

Book Cliffs, Utah.

Sunset on the Hoodoos formations, south of Farmington, New Mexico.

Sandstone pinnacles, the Needles, Canyonlands National Park, Utah.

They don't look like badlands. They look like the flaky, fragrant, lard crusts that the Mother Goose bakers laid over their fairy-tale pies, or like candle tallow collecting at the bases of peach-scented candles. If you put an ocean over them, they would make a reasonable ocean floor, which they once were. No crags, no peaks, no crevasses. They are just friendly mounds of sandstone. But if you want to get across them in a reasonable amount of time, go around.

86

Coral sand dunes, Utah State Park, near Kanab, Utah.

Bryce Canyon National Park and Pariah-Vermillion Cliffs, Utah.

Much of the Colorado Plateau is a sandcastle that was built to last. You can duplicate the process with sand and water, which is all that sandcastles are. When you wet the sand and compress it, it holds a shape. At most beaches there are annual sandcastle competitions. The best builders might attempt the avant-garde, and reconstruct Bryce Canyon in amazing detail. A couple of days of waves and wind will turn it back to sand, just like the real thing, only on the beach it doesn't take as long.

Afternoon, Lake Powell, Glen Canyon National Recreation Area.

LAKE POWELL

Phil, having served in the Navy in Southeast Asian waters in the 1960s, had apparently had enough of running boats. So it was I, the landlubber artilleryman, who, at Phil's gracious insistence, stood at the control console, receiving a brief lesson in houseboat propulsion and navigation from a clean-cut young dockhand named Kevin.

This was a fifty-foot houseboat, set on long pontoons, tied up at Hall's Crossing Marina on Lake Powell's southern shore. The two families, Phil's and mine, eight of us in all, had engaged the houseboat for a week of cruising on Powell's waters, and into her canyons. Up the dock, two more families from our Southern California neighborhood were installing themselves in another fifty-footer, the largest available. We aimed to make a week of it. Among us, the four families had brought provisions for, oh, fifty or sixty people. It was all stowed in huge ice chests fore and aft, and in the refrigerators in the comfortable galleys.

Lake Powell was created (when the Glen Canyon Dam at Page was finished in 1963) for a number of practical, political, and recreational reasons, but across the Southwest the lake has become associated mainly with one word: *houseboat*. Some people rent houseboats, which are available in three sizes, at one of the five marinas. Other people, who tend to live closer to the lake, keep their own houseboats—beautiful, luxurious things, inevitably envied by users of the rental fleet—moored in private slips.

Our humble houseboat was just fine, with all the amenities of a well-equipped mobile home. For stark juxtaposition of civilization with antiquity, I will argue there is no place starker than Lake Powell, where tiny motorized islands of upscale comfort (some complete with satellite dish) move about remote, inhabitant-resistant geology that was hardly accessible in the million years before 1963.

The region's difficult accessibility had started coming clear to me earlier in the day, when the four families in land caravan from San Diego turned off Utah Highway 95, the Bicentennial Highway, onto Route 276, the last leg to the marina. We were well into our second day of travel from Southern California, and my mind had begun to run somewhat on faith way back at Mexican Hat, as the pavement got narrower and the landscape more forbidding. We turned off U.S. 163 onto U.S. 191, then after a while turned left onto State 95, and forty miles later turned left onto Route 276, at which point I figured that the lake had to be right around the corner. Thirty miles later, I announced that going to Lake Powell was a real "carrot trip"—the destination forever dangling out there just beyond reach. When eventually, beyond a long washboard landscape of sandstone dunes, I unmistakably spotted water, I gurgled some happy exclamation of surprise.

In minutes we were at the marina, hauling provisions in carts, which the marina thoughtfully supplied, down to the boats. Hall's Crossing was a curious oasis, as mercantile as a small shopping center, but ninety-five water miles up the lake from the nearest real civilization, at Page, Arizona. At Hall's was the marina, a store, a cafe, some camp facilities, an airstrip, and, around a bend, an auto ferry across the lake to the Bullfrog Marina, which served houseboaters coming to Powell from points north.

The dockhands were young men and women, clean-cut, with the appearance of students working for the summer. There was about the place a drive-in-restaurant urbanity that was downright incongruous, so near the middle of nowhere.

It was July, and breezy-hot—desert heat—on the boats. Kevin showed me the throttles that controlled twin sixty-horsepower outboards hung on the tails of the pontoons. By correctly manipulating the engines, I, the captain, could maneuver the big vessel in the close quarters of Powell's arms and canyons. To make a sharp left, for example, I could back the left engine while advancing the right engine. At the dock, it sounded simple. Kevin showed me, just in case, a spare propeller stowed beneath the console. After a couple of practice turns, we dropped Kevin on the dock and said we would see him in a week. Under Captain Grant's tentative command, we headed out to open sea, cutting a tableau that would have stupefied John Wesley Powell.

Much about modernity would have stupefied John Wesley Powell. He was not given even to the meager leisures of his own era. Powell, fighting on the Union side, lost an arm in the Civil War at the Battle of Shiloh. Nevertheless he remained in service, commanding artillery, until the war's end.

Powell was a scholar and a geologist, but he seems to have been driven mainly by the restive itch of the frontiersman. He was perfectly suited to exploring, and he found the West rewarding territory. He took it into his head to explore the Green and Colorado rivers by boat, a dangerous and unprecedented notion. In those days the rivers ran free and unmanaged and very wild, from their Wyoming and Colorado headwaters to the Gulf of California.

Men knew about the rivers and their deep canyons, first the Native Americans who lived along the Colorado, and later the Spanish explorers and the first Anglo settlers. Along Glen Canyon, the Anasazi Indians, who lived in the area before A.D. 800, worked their way down to the fertile riverbank at places where the chasm widened and the descent was gentler.

But unimaginable geologic forces had created this terrain. What, eons before, had been an ocean floor was thrust upward by forces still giving the planet its final form. Down from the towering mountains to the northeast came the waters of a young and powerful river, cutting through the sandstone and leaving behind deep, precipitous gorges that even primitive people knew were better left alone. Until one-armed John Wesley Powell came along with his boat idea, men had never been down in there.

Powell and his party set out from Green River, Wyoming, on May 24, 1869. They came out below the Grand Canyon on August 30, minus four of the party who had deserted beyond the canyon rim, preferring to face hostile Indians rather than more white water. Three of the four deserters were killed by the Indians. They were the adventure's only fatalities, and the irony of their demise has been told countless times since.

Powell the geologist kept careful journals that told some of the earliest stories of the earth's geology, as recorded and revealed in the strata of the canyon walls. He made another trip in 1871, acquiring more data. Powell, an archconservationist, became aware of the need to manage water in the arid West, and he might have approved of the Glen Canyon Dam and the lake in his name. But Powell would have rolled his eyes at the thought of refrigerator-equipped houseboats plying the lake, piloted by shirtless, shoeless revelers toting provisions for sixty.

The irony here is that people use houseboats very much to go exploring. We maneuvered expertly into a number of fascinating canyons, and from the decks spent hours observing and remarking on geologic and physical curiosities.

The most appreciated of these curiosities, at least to me, was the way that red and blue reinforce each other in the color spectrum. The red sandstone gave the sky a blue intensity usually seen only at altitudes near the edge of space. That blue, in turn, infused the sandstone with husky rusts and roses that had the vibrancy of blooms, as if the rock were alive. We traveled in a vivid, banded world, blue water meeting red terrain meeting blue sky.

The scope of our exploring was limited by the lake's size (vast), and the boat's speed (tedious) and fuel thirst (voracious). (There was also the regular need to stop and fish and swim and whittle away at the provisions mountain. It was a life I would recommend to anyone.)

The lake reaches about 190 miles from the dam in Arizona to the northeast, beyond the remote Hite's Marina, and its numerous arms and canyons add up to about 1,900 miles of shoreline, longer than the U.S. Pacific coast.

We had planned to visit Rainbow Arch, the largest natural stone bridge on earth, advertised as the lake's most famous landmark. But we didn't figure on the distances. Hall's Crossing was at milepost 95, Rainbow Arch near milepost 49. If we had set our course immediately toward it, we might have made the trip in a week. Instead we waddled north and east for a day or two. Though we did eventually turn south with the idea of going to Rainbow, we only reached the Escalante Arm, at milepost 68, before abandoning the effort. Next time we may plan better. In the meantime,

I believe that Rainbow Arch, famous as it is, would have to go some to compare to the genuine landmark, which is the lake itself.

We quickly acquired the Lake Powell docking technique, nosing the boat perpendicular to the shore and tying up with lines played out from port and starboard quarters. The boaters moored almost exclusively in the canyons, where the choicest spots featured a bit of gently sloping, sandstone-smooth shoreline beneath soaring, weather-streaked cliff faces. The best spots, everywhere we went on the lake, were marked by pairs of shallow grooves at the waterline, worn there by houseboat pontoons rubbing gently against the sandstone in the night.

The houseboats had bunks for eight, but it was hot, so we hauled the bunk mats and sleeping bags to the wide roof and slept up there under the stars. At night the cliff faces above us stood inky-black against the stars, giving the strongest impression of a hole in the sky. One night, beyond a canyon rim, we watched lightning flash. Though the lightning was not very distant, the thunder didn't reach us, deep in our canyon. We felt protected, and in fact we were. I recalled instructions given us at the marina to get off the open lake if it looked like some weather might be coming up. That particular storm, we learned later, capsized a couple of houseboats caught out in the open.

The canyons twisted so that, even though several boats might populate a canyon, each could find solitude at a moorage around the bend. At times the silence roared in our ears. Twilights and nightfall were extremely romantic. I told my teenaged daughter Jessica that when she was thirty-five and old enough to marry, she must come here for her honeymoon and with her new husband rent a houseboat just for two and drink champagne on the roof of their houseboat, enfolded in these canyons in the thundering silence of twilight.

In most places we could step off the houseboats and walk the shores or climb into the rocks. We found many shady, archlike "windows" worn by time and weather into the base of soaring

91

cliffs. Some of these cliff faces were so high that they seemed to bend over us, like an orchestra shell.

It was sobering, sitting down in the cool of the evening to steak and corn on the cob, to imagine the people who once populated these canyon rims, existing on grains and berries and game, and living very much on the ground. At Defiance House in Forgotten Canyon, we climbed a narrow, winding trail to a restoration of dwellings occupied by these people, the Anasazi, eight or nine centuries ago. The mud dwellings and a circular, ceremonial kiva were built beneath a wide, protecting overhang, well below the canyon rim. It would have been a place easily defended. In that era there was not a lake surface a few feet down the trail, but a drop of hundreds of feet. On the cliff face above the ruins, petroglyphs by an ancient artist show three armed human figures in combat.

The ancient figures gave an account of circumstances in the time of the Anasazi, but they spoke mainly to a larger topic, to the grandeur of the Southwest. Humans come, forge their successes, fight their battles, leave their mark, and go. The great plateau remains, an eternal contract of land with sky and day with night, breeding its own life, with only the seasonal cycles to suggest the passing of time. Now other people come, in the late twentieth century, marking their considerable presence not with petroglyphs but with great dams and vast lakes. But when and if these people should go, the plateau will remain, and the great dams and lakes will become only the mark of a primitive people carried forward for inspection by the advanced people of a future time.

In the context of the plateau it is possible to encounter moments of intense personal privacy. I suspect that was as true in the time of the Anasazi as it is now. I can easily suppose that an Anasazi counterpart might have watched the sunrise—the desert's most beautiful hour, I think—and felt the same wholeness flooding from within. It was the promise of this encounter that stirred me awake by dawn each morning. The desert never let me down. Others must have felt as I did, and one memorable morning brought a moment of sweet collaboration.

We were in Iceberg Canyon, tied up in a little bay along a pleasant shore under a towering cliff. Although our little bay was completely in shade, the canyon walls opposite were brilliant with morning light. The earth was perfectly still. Then into this stillness, from beyond the bend, came the disembodied notes of a trumpet.

The song was "Amazing Grace." The trumpeter was very good. The notes were precise and rang like crystal. There was no echo. The canyon's natural acoustics moved the notes effortlessly across the distance. I thought the song probably could be clearly heard in heaven. It was a remarkable event, and easily the most beautiful music I ever heard.

I never saw the trumpeter. By the time of our departure, the shoreline in that direction was vacant. If you told me the trumpeter beyond the bend was God, I think I would probably believe you.

On the water at sunset, Lake Powell near the Escalante River.

Four families embarked on two fifty-foot houseboats out of Hall's Crossing Marina on Lake Powell, with enough provisions to sail to China, and too much beauty all around to be divided into days. The families steered their houseboats into an anchorage on an evening such as this, with the prospect of distant lightning and the Milky Way in the night sky ahead. A father tugged his teenaged daughter aside and said, "I don't give many orders, but when you are thirty-five and old enough to get married, you and your husband will come back here for your honeymoon."

94

Forest waterfall, Oak Creek Canyon, central Arizona.

The first four elements identified by humans were earth, fire, air, and water, and the most restless of these was water. The earth changed slowly with the seasons; fire came and went; and the air was erratic. But water was always on the move, or trying hard to be, whether there was a lot of it or a little. Raindrops slid off leaves and pine needles; rivulets gathered on the forest floor and came together as brooks, which rushed down to meet the streams, the water gathering energy as it went, and growing louder. The water was never quiet, day or night. When humans tried to pen it up, it sought and found escape. Eventually humans learned to tap water's energy by building pens that would release the water a little at a time. The water rushed against the new dam and swirled behind it, rising to go over it, appeased by the periodic release from below, creating a long, deep reservoir of energy so vast and resolute that even the best engineers knew their efforts were temporary.

Falls and grotto, Zion National Park, Utah.

96

Forbidding Canyon, Lake Powell, near Rainbow Bridge National Monument.

Indian ruins above Escalante Arm, Lake Powell.

Even today, with easy access to Lake Powell from north and south, and with houseboats sending out battery-powered compact-disc music in all directions, explorers come upon scene after scene of silence so complete that they want to hold their breath, lest they disturb the water. Sound carries extremely well, with great clarity, through Glen Canyon's loops and arms and channels. And where sound carries best, silences become louder also. The acoustics in Glen Canyon are the same that you would encounter in a great symphony hall.

Sunset, Dead Horse Point State Park, Utah.

Sandstone grotto sculpted by water, near Glen Canyon, Utah.

Of all the billions of earth sunsets, no two are ever alike, with one major exception: all of them have followed a strict schedule. Humans have found that schedule so interesting that they have learned to time it to the minute. They publish it in their newspapers every day, along with schedules for sunrise, moonrise, moonset, the quarters of the moon, the movements of the planets and stars, and the coming and going of the tides. What we regard as natural beauty is actually a series of events carefully orchestrated to repeat a pattern. The miracle of earth is that within that pattern exist infinite opportunities for variation. No two snowflakes are alike, except to have six spokes. No two gorgeous sunsets are alike, except to arrive on schedule. Sandstone grottos share a crystalline geology, though the sandstone's grain is clearly its own.

Light at the bend, Slickhorn Canyon, Utah.

So earth events follow a schedule.
Suppose those events punched a clock?
Suppose with every sunset the wind
and rain and rivers fell into repose
until dawn, recovering strength for the
next day's work. What would the earth
look like today? Hard to imagine, but
no harder than knowing that rivers
carved out the gorges a pebble at a
time, as many by night as by day. The
earth is a work in progress, done by an
artist who rubs diligently against a rock
sculpture until the flakes come away,
one by one, and the sculpture is always
one moment nearer completion. It is
hard to understand such care. It is hard
to fall asleep by the sea, listening to the
pounding surf, thinking that in a
billion years or more the pounding,
night or day, has never ceased.

101

Snow on the Goosenecks, San Juan River, Utah.

102

Sunset at Red Rock Crossing, near Sedona, Arizona.

This is not trick photography. The red rock spires really are incandescent. When enough sunlight is absorbed, energy sources within the rock are triggered, and the spires begin to glow. And there really is a brilliant light source deep within the walls of Zion shining like a tiny local sun. The phenomena are there, plain for the eye to see. The tricks are nature's—two more examples of those common Southwestern situations in which the observers simply have to believe their eyes. The photographer's only trick is capturing these sights on film.

Sunset, Kolob section, Zion National Park, Utah.

Painted Desert Inn from Kachina Point, near old Highway 66, Arizona.

ROUTE 66

On my desk—well, we can't really say "desk," anymore. That word conjures up pictures of wide, oak mesas of thought rising from tile floors in vaulted Southwestern studies with casement windows overlooking shady verandas and purple vistas beyond. What we have today are "work stations," vertical prefabricated assemblies in which are positioned the elements—keyboard, monitor, memory discs, printer—that drive the engines of modern communication. It gives up something in romance. A work station, conjuring images of Wall Street offices and launch control centers, will never be consistent with the Southwestern ambience, indoors or out. We suffer them, however (all but the resolute purists) because when compared to the grand desk and the venerable, romantic Underwood, work stations streamline the creative process, improving mental efficiency, the very thought process, by about twenty-five percent, which leaves more time for strolling on the veranda.

So. I am sitting at my work station, and on the prefabricated shelf above the monitor sits a piece of history, about thumbnail-sized, red and flinty with sharp edges. It is a macadam fragment from old U.S. Route 66. I obtained it by illegal means.

My wife and I were driving west from Tucumcari to Flagstaff, following Interstate 40 but thinking about old Route 66, the storied highway—they called it The Main Street of America—that reached through the middle of this century southwest from Chicago to Oklahoma, then west across the Texas Panhandle, through northern New Mexico and Arizona to the Pacific Ocean at Santa Monica.

Later on that June afternoon we arrived at the turnoff for the Petrified Forest and the Painted Desert. We were not about to skip the Painted Desert. In this world there are two kinds of motorists: those who take side trips, and those who want to "get there." I happen to know that a "get-there" person can in time evolve into a side-tripper; in the late sixties and early seventies, I made the run more than once from Abilene, Texas, to San Diego in a little more than nineteen hours, stopping for gas, Fritos, and coffee in combination with calls of nature.

In my "get-there" mode, in daylight the Southwest to me appeared flat, featureless and—along some stretches—endless. And that was a shame. The "get-there" people never see anything but

Indian symbol above right; rain serpent.

their own driveways at home, not many of which have ever been designated as national parks or historic places. Among my wife's favorite stories is of one of her elders, driving years ago with his wife east from the Grand Canyon toward Tennessee. The wife said something like, "Oh, look, that sign says only three miles to the Painted Desert."

"Gmpf," said the husband, and hammered on.

In the visitor center, just north off the interstate, the ranger gave me a park map. "A few hundred feet beyond the entrance station, you will see a line of old telephone poles without any wires," she said. "Just follow the park road beyond them to the Painted Desert overlooks."

I asked what the old telephone poles were, and she said they followed the old route of U.S. 66. At the entrance station we paid our five-dollar entry fee, and the ranger there, a pleasant woman with an accommodating smile, reminded us of federal law prohibiting the collection of any petrified wood.

We stopped where the line of old telephone poles intersected the park road. They marched in a long, picket-line reach, off to the east and to the west, following the route of old U.S. 66. Somewhere nearby lay the old roadway, obscured now by desert growth of many seasons. I looked east and west down the long line of poles disappearing into the desert and felt very much at the center of a vast distance. It was a feeling that belonged entirely to another time. The interstates and today's cars have made it obsolete.

I stood looking east across the horizon toward Gallup, Albuquerque, Tucumcari, and beyond. It was from that direction that the highway came. U.S. 66 was the brainchild of an Oklahoma businessman named Cyrus Avery, who by the 1920s already had a clear vision of the role that good roads and paved highways would play in the American experience.

Though a national highway system was created in 1926, the actual routing and paving of roads remained very political. The federal government realized the need for a system to replace the old network of "trails" that had been established during the 1800s by local government agencies and public "associations." There were many compelling reasons for a good system of roads. Farmers could reach the markets. Mail could reach the farmers. The railroads' interstate commerce monopoly could be broken. But more compelling than any other reason was this: Americans were becoming very fond of their newfangled automobiles and the freedom they represented. But that freedom was not complete without good roads to drive on.

Washington approved final routes and provided matching funds but left it to the states to decide routes and set priorities for getting the work done. Road-paving technology was new and very expensive. States and counties had to be convinced that the roads would be worth it. Much boosterism, from Tulsa to Kingman, accompanied the construction of U.S. 66. Avery and others had created the U.S. 66 Highway Association, which moved its meetings from town to town along the route.

Through most of the 1930s, the highway through the Southwest was a patchwork of pavement and gravel. Most of the work was done with equipment drawn by horses and mules. In many counties, citizens formed volunteer work teams. Frequently the road bent around even small hills instead of cutting through, because construction was faster—the great earth-moving machines of today didn't exist then—and much cheaper. In Arizona the paving went along all right, but the state was reluctant to build expensive bridges. Instead the pavement followed the contours of washes and arroyos, making for trouble when it rained.

Late in 1937 paving was completed across New Mexico and Arizona, and U.S. 66 was completed from Chicago to Los Angeles. The highway was poured in sixty-foot sections, in two lanes, each lane nine feet wide. The technology was new, and money tight, and the original highway was not as durable as it would become. The traffic on it was immediate, beginning with the great Dust Bowl migration, then expanding tourism, and then World War II.

106

Movements of men and materiel during the war ate the highway alive. Widening and repaving, now with asphalt in many places, was already under way by the late 1940s. By the 1950s, plans for an interstate system were being drawn.

Short stretches of the original highway survive. We had driven such a stretch, just east of Elk City, Oklahoma. The paving joints, as we drove at 55 mph, slapped in a hard rhythm against the tires. From the late 1930s to the 1960s, these two nine-foot lanes—one westbound, one eastbound—carried traffic at speeds averaging maybe 45 mph. I traveled that way in my youth, languishing in the heat of the back seat, wondering how many trucks really *were* in front of us. Standing now on the old highway, with eighteen-wheelers thrumming past on the adjacent interstate, I could no longer picture that speed of travel.

But I could picture the billboards. For such a scenic wonderland, the Southwest, in the time that I have known it, certainly has turned over a lot of roadside space to billboards. The arriving highways picked up the Southwest tourist routes first opened up by the railroads. U.S. 66 became a thriving corridor of business, full of tourists arriving to witness Southwest grandeur for themselves. Unlike patrons of the old Fred Harvey railroad tours, the auto travelers were free to pick and choose where they ate, where they slept, where they shopped, and what sights they saw. Albuquerque, Grants, Gallup, Holbrook, Winslow, Flagstaff, and the other U.S. 66 communities prospered with the tourist dollars arriving with each car from the east. Up went roadside motels, gas stations, and curio shops. And up went the billboards. A Flagstaff sign painter named Jack Fuss made a good living and a colorful reputation by building and painting huge billboards across Arizona and New Mexico that would become, for tourists, a Southwestern signature as lasting as the Grand Canyon.

Remnants of the old boards remain, like faded hieroglyphs of an invading tribe. This sounds like ancient history. But believe me, I am not an old man, and the U.S. 66 paving was completed only five years before I was born. The completed highway was less than twenty years old when my family drove it to the Grand Canyon for the first time. The towns at night were alive with neon and romance, shiny baubles of air-conditioned civilization strung on a slender necklace of concrete and asphalt.

The necklace has become a conveyor belt now, on which the movement never stops, or hardly even slows. From beneath the old line of telephone poles I watched the interstate traffic whizzing along, half a mile away. It occurred to me that all the vehicles on the interstate between Chicago and Los Angeles at that moment, plunked down on old U.S. 66, would line up bumper-to-bumper in both directions between the two cities. At that moment, almost sunset on the Painted Desert, I watched the highway and saw congestion, and with it felt a sense of loss.

The park road, as we followed it, turned west and then south past Painted Desert vistas, then back toward the interstate, where the road once again intersected the old poles. I felt compelled to stop, get out, and search. The poles were numbered, with metal numbers like house numbers. The pole just west of the park road was number 7017. I took a picture of it and walked west through dry desert brush, noting the tracks of desert creature activity, toward pole number 7018. North of the line, about hundred feet away, I thought I saw a raised profile, like a roadbed. I made my way to it, and onto it, and saw, scattered in the brush, chunks of old asphalt. This must have been the old road. I looked east and west again, knowing I had crossed this place before. The sense of distance returned, and it felt good. I laughed at the memory of being stopped not far from this spot by Arizona troopers. We—me, my mother, grandmother, and aunts—were returning to Texas from a California trip in 1954, two years before Eisenhower signed the bill that begat the nearby interstate. I was eleven, and my mother was at the wheel. My tender ears were not permitted in the chambers of the justice of the peace at Holbrook, but I learned later that the J.P., when he said, "Thirty dollars or thirty days,"

107

loosed a tide of invective from my grandmother that nearly got us all arrested. We had to wire home for the thirty dollars. We didn't see the Painted Desert that trip.

I poked around in the roadbed and found, partially buried in sand, a triangular piece of asphalt, macadam-encrusted, weighing about five pounds. Furtively, I picked it up, dusted it off, returned along the roadbed to the car, and placed the asphalt in the trunk. We turned around and followed the park road back to the entrance station, where we heeded a sign to "Stop." The park ranger smiled benignly and said, "Did you pick up anything off the ground that you didn't put back?"

"Yes," I said, half by admission and half thinking no one would care, or maybe one-quarter by admission, and three-quarters of the other. "I picked up an asphalt chunk of old Highway 66."

The ranger's smiled turned apologetic, matching her description of rules and telephone calls to higher authorities and possible fines and so forth. I willingly parked the car, opened the trunk, and retrieved the asphalt. As I did, my thumb found a piece of red, flinty macadam that wiggled in its asphalt seat like a loose tooth. I wiggled it some more. Darned if it didn't fall out of its asphalt seat, back into the trunk of the car. I closed the trunk, carried the asphalt chunk back to the window, and with a smile to match hers, relinquished it to the ranger.

In the visitor center I found that old Highway 66 had inspired not only songs, novels, and television shows, but a biography, title *Route 66*, with text by Susan Croce Kelly and a photo essay by Quinta Scott. Naturally a whole chapter was devoted to billboards, making the book, for me, authentic.

Merchants still put up billboards in the Southwest, and some of them are huge, but they are not as creative as they used to be. My wife and I remembered the famous jackrabbit "Here It Is" bill-

board, and I remembered the "Running Indian" billboards, and Whiting Brothers gas station signs that were two hundred feet wide. My wife had just been describing the "For Men Winslow Arizona" billboard, which I vaguely remembered, when we reached the Painted Desert visitor center and my *Route 66* book discovery. Almost immediately in the billboard chapter, she turned to a "For Men" billboard photo, a curvy, quasi-abstract cowgirl in silhouette, suggesting that Winslow possessed attractions to lure even the "get-there" men.

In fact the billboard was placed (along roadsides clear to New York City) by the creative proprietors of a men's clothing store in downtown Winslow. The billboards repeated the store's marquee, which was cut out in the curvy girl's silhouette and outlined in neon.

The store had long since closed. At Winslow we exited the interstate and cruised the old highway, which was separated into one-way streets through town, wondering if we could find the old building. After a couple of loops, we parked at a curb to get our bearings. We looked at a Winslow street photo in *Route 66* and saw in it a couple of distinctive features—highway signs, building shapes—that were right in front of us.

We were parked right in front of the building. Now it was called the Eddie G. Chacon Clothing Company. We backed up and looked up at the marquee. It was painted over now, but there, unmistakably, was the cowgirl's curvy silhouette. It was a stirring find.

Flagstaff was booked practically solid with summer tourists headed for the Grand Canyon. We found a room across the highway from the railroad tracks. Santa Fe freights rolled all night. I lay awake, imagining my arrest for gravel rustling, knowing what my grandmother would say.

108

Ruins at Puerco site, Petrified Forest National Park, Arizona.

From A.D. 1100 to 1400 a branch of the Anasazi culture carried on business along the Puerco River, in what is now the Petrified Forest National Park. Obviously it was a primitive lifestyle, but the Anasazi's building skill is still evident seven hundred years later, at this pueblo south of the river. This building is laid out like an ancient motel, except for a swimming pool. Building skills have become somewhat more sophisticated since then, though it is interesting to travel nearby Interstate 40 and look at some of the motels. Will they still be standing after three hundred years? And will the skill that went into them still be evident seven hundred years later?

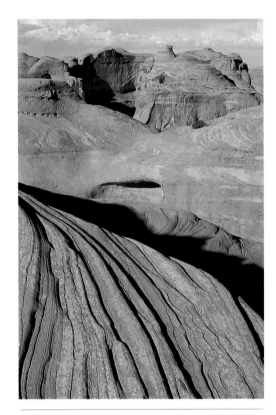

The railroads in the late 1800s, and the highway system beginning in the 1920s opened up the Southwest to the general American population. People came in huge numbers, drawn by reports of the magnificent canyon in Arizona and the beauty and native allure of the American Southwest. And when they arrived, they found that the Southwest was all that had been promised. But until they came, they could only imagine the circumstances of living on what was still considered a wild frontier. They would have been surprised at the extremes to which people went to survive in this land. What the newcomers didn't yet understand was the Southwestern natives' belief that they and the earth were one. This land was their altar.

Rock forms at Hunt Mesa, Monument Valley Tribal Park, Arizona. Wood-covered Navajo hogan, Monument Valley Tribal Park, Arizona.

112

Grand Canyon Railroad departing Grand Canyon Village, Arizona.

The railroad is still a good way—sometimes the only way—to get to the Grand Canyon in wintertime. Santa Fe built a spur off its main line up to the canyon around the turn of the century. Roads and highways were mostly unpaved then, and automobiles were still curiosities. The first trains, in the early 1900s, cut four hours off the travel time from Flagstaff to the Grand Canyon. The number of visitors to the canyon skyrocketed, and amenities for them were developed along the South Rim. Today, vintage steam trains make daily round trips from a restored pine-log depot at Williams. Even in winter the destination is stunning.

Winter snows on the South Rim, Grand Canyon.

114

The Hopi House at the Grand Canyon was not designed and built by the Hopi culture, but by a young woman from Minneapolis. Her name was Mary Colter, and she designed buildings for the Fred Harvey Company. As tourism became an industry in the Southwest, and accommodations started to be built, design became an issue. It was a natural impulse to bring design with you from the East, in railroad depots and guest buildings. Colter challenged that impulse with her buildings at the Grand Canyon and with her Santa Fe depots and hotels along the main line. Many tourist events across the Southwest now take place in buildings, plazas, and courtyards that have evolved from native and old-European blueprints that were in place two hundred years before the railroad's arrival.

Hopi House, Grand Canyon National Park, Arizona.

Courtyard and art galleries, Tlaquepaque Village, Sedona, Arizona.

116

Wigwam Motel and '37 Ford along old Route 66, Holbrook, Arizona.

Historic highway sign and the 66 Diner, New Mexico.

Paving was completed all the way from Chicago to Los Angeles in 1938, and U.S. Route 66 became "The Main Street of America." The highway created a population boom in Southern California and brought a great deal of money into the Southwest. Highway 66 was actually a strip industry, 2,200 miles long. Americans, thrilled with the new freedom that auto travel represented, were eager to hit the road. Their destinations were Santa Fe, the Painted Desert, the Grand Canyon, and California, but along the route, merchants knew that every arriving car could mean money for the town. Competition was lively and creative among owners of gas stations, motels, cafes, and curio shops. By the 1960s, interstate highways were starting to bypass most of those merchants. But Americans from the earlier generation carried with them into middle and old age memories of that highway with its colorful billboards, and of the motels and cafes and curiosities that fulfilled the billboards' promises.

118

Storm clouds, Laguna Indian Reservation, New Mexico.

New Mexico enjoys (for those who dote on sky drama) a greater frequency of thunderstorms than any other state except Florida. That is because New Mexico sits at the confluence of weather currents off the Great Plains, off the Rocky Mountains, and up from the Gulf of Mexico. This confluence occurs above a topography that embraces six of the seven life zones and is so jumbled that forms of vegetation and conditions of climate may be found at elevations where those forms and conditions shouldn't be. The results are interesting to scientists, and fascinating to observers, particularly those who like weather.

Comb Ridge in storm light, proposed San Juan Anasazi Wilderness Area, Utah.

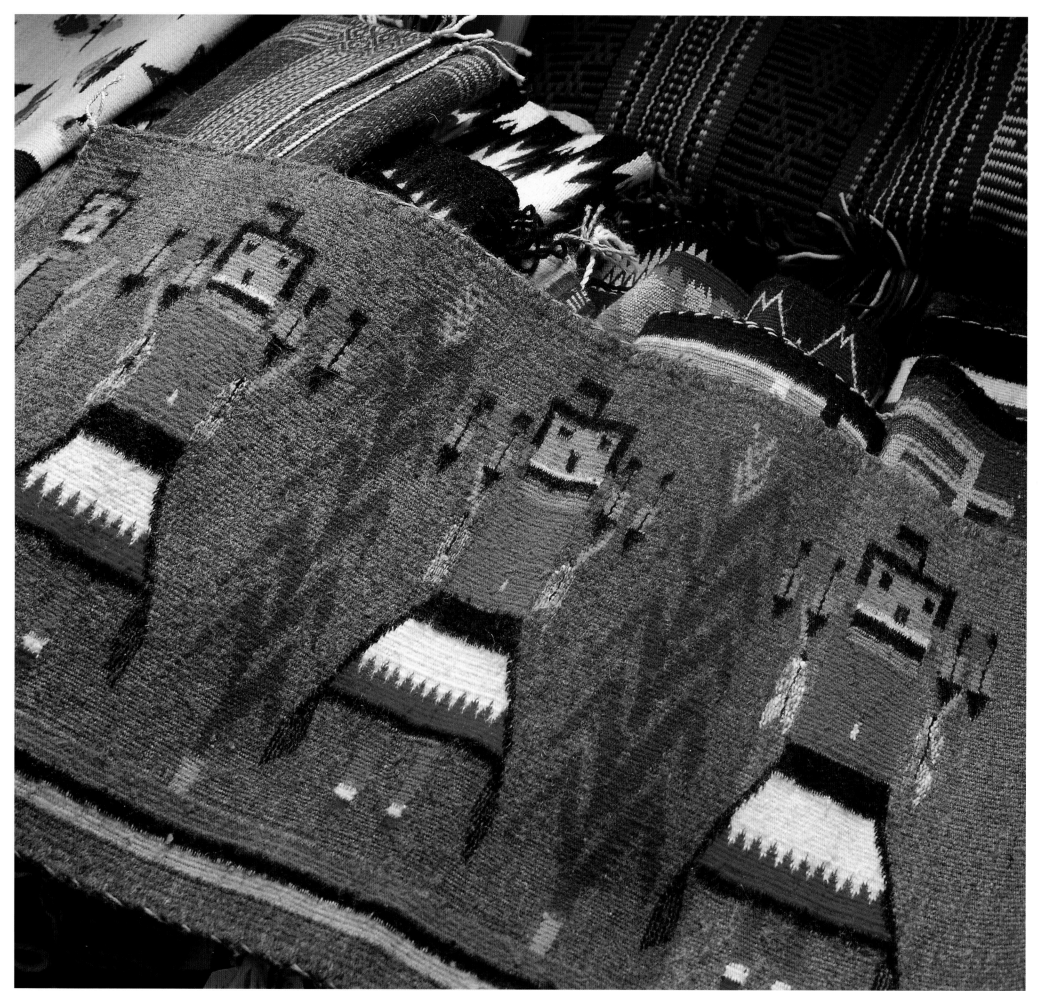

Navajo rugs for sale at Hubbell Trading Post, Ganado, northeast Arizona.

TRADING POST

In the rug room at the historic Hubbell Trading Post in northeast Arizona are stacked hundreds of beautiful Indian rugs, worth hundreds of thousands of dollars. Bill Malone, when the pace of business allows, likes to go back to the rug room, recline on a stack of rugs, put his feet up, and shoot the breeze with visitors.

"Most of the clientele are tourists now," said Malone, Hubbell's trader-manager. "But, well, there's a ninety-year-old gramma waiting to pay her bill right now. And there's another one, just walked in; she's about eighty-five."

The two ladies were Navajo, one from Ganado—the town where Hubbell's is located—and the other from Chinle, the gateway community to Canyon de Chelly National Monument, thirty miles north. In Window Rock, Arizona, twenty-five miles to the east on a good, straight highway, sits Basha's, as big and fine and brightly lit and well-stocked a modern supermarket as you would find in Scottsdale. The ladies preferred to buy their groceries over the counter at tiny Hubbell's, where the light comes from windows and bare hundred-watt bulbs, and whose tall, plank shelves hold the basics.

The Navajo and Hopi tribes have been doing business at Hubbell's and other northeastern Arizona trading posts since the 1800s. In those days the Indians brought items of value—baskets, jewelry, woven blankets, hides, wool—to the trader and in return received goods—food, tools, cloth. Today the transactions are less romantic.

"Most of it is money these days," said Malone, a slightly built, amiable man whose even, easy voice has borrowed from the Navajo cadences he knows so well. Every day he buys something from the Indians, but "if there's any goods involved, it's kind of a plus, or an add-on—'in excess of,' something like that."

But the nature of the business—fair exchange—has remained the same for a hundred years. "I bought two rugs yesterday from a mother and a daughter from Cedar Ridge, which is up by Page, which is a three-hour drive from here," said Malone. "If you pay fair, you'll get people to bring you things."

Fairness is, of course, an expression of harmony, and harmony is the moral and spiritual engine that drives the Native American civilization. J.L. Hubbell, by operating on those principles, became not only merchant but friend to the Navajo, after he opened his trading post at Ganado in 1880. Hubbell wore thick eyeglasses in round, black frames, so naturally the Navajo nicknamed him Wearing Spectacles. But in the third person, they called him naalyehe ya sidaho, a "person who sits for things of value," and they called his store Naalyehe ba hooghan, or "a house with things of value." Hubbell brought modern goods to the Navajo, but he ran his store in the ancient ways, which means that in essence the customers ran the store. Indian trading was and is an extremely deliberate activity, paced by a rhythm in which the concept of "hour" has no meaning. The trader's most valuable commodity was patience.

"If you tried to get in the fast lane," said Bill Malone, "you wouldn't last long out here."

Malone, who grew up in Gallup, has entered his fourth decade as a trader, first at Pinon, a village at the end of the pavement deep in the Navajo Reservation's interior, and later at Hubbell's. His formal training, in college and military service, was in electronics.

"I couldn't find a tube-changing job, so I got into the trading business," he said. "I've liked it ever since." Malone married a Navajo, Minnie Goodluck Malone, and they have five children who, as Malone said, "are married to Navajos."

Malone has no relationship to the Hubbell family, who operated the post for almost ninety years, after which the post was designated a National Historical Site. The National Park Service owns the site, beneath cottonwood trees flanking the Pueblo Colorado Wash.

"When the job came open, I applied for it," said Malone. "The site is operated by Southwest Parks and Monuments, which is a nonprofit cooperative association. After all the expenses are figured up, they donate the profits back to the Park Service."

The village of Ganado—so named by J.L. Hubbell to honor his old Indian friend and nineteenth-century associate Ganado Mucho—is forty-four miles north of Interstate 40, at the intersec-

tion of U.S. Highway 191 and State Highway 264 in far eastern Arizona. Hubbell's lies at the end of a dirt lane off Highway 264. The store appears as it always did, a rock building that houses the three-room trading post, and to the east a large barn and corrals, mostly unused. In another time, all the customers arrived in wagons or on horseback, and livestock were items of trade. Practically no one arrives on a horse anymore, and Malone does not trade in livestock.

"The tribe has its livestock auction right here in Ganado," said Malone. "You can get more money just taking your wool to the tribe now, since the tribe deals directly with the buyers."

The post's front door opens into the general store, an old, shady place whose walls are lined to the high ceiling with plank shelves that hold canned goods, household wares, bolts of cloth, and—in this modern day—boxes and boxes of sneakers. The open, middle area of the room was the "bullpen," where in the old days customers socialized around the Franklin stove and contemplated the fairness of a proposed trade. The store keeps a sense of cozy clutteredness. A narrow doorway leads to the post's crafts room, some of which is office space, and through another door on the left is the rug room. Outside, in the dirt parking lot, may be parked cars, vans, and campers from any of the fifty states. Tour buses show up regularly, from Albuquerque, Phoenix, or California.

"We're kinda the stopping point between Canyon de Chelly and the Petrified Forest," said Malone.

The first Southwestern Indian trading posts date to the return of the Navajo from their internment in eastern New Mexico from 1863 to 1868, at a place called Bosque Redondo. The internment was imposed by the United States government to quell Navajo raiding habits. The result was devastation of the Navajo culture and economy. They had done excellent weaving from before the time of the Spaniards. On their return to the reservation, with livestock allotments from the government, they resumed weaving, and traded blankets and wool for food, housewares, tack, and tools at the posts that sprang up around Dinetah, as the Navajos call their wide, majestic country.

The first trading post was built of native stone and operated by a German, Hermann Wolf, on the Little Colorado River east and north of Flagstaff. Wolf died in 1899, but the post continued in operation into the 1900s under subsequent owners, until one of these owners one day exhibited an astonishing flash of cultural ignorance. In the store, he put on display a skull that he had recovered from a nearby archaeological dig. What to an Anglo represented a macabre curiosity, to the Navajo represented the "death spirit," or chindii, which haunts all persons and places it touches. The Navajo never traded at the store again.

Another story, maybe just lore, tells of a customer, a Navajo, suffering an epileptic seizure inside a trading post. The trader immediately gathered the victim under the shoulders and dragged him outside, not for fresh air but because the trader knew what would happen if anyone died in his store. Novelist Tony Hillerman, who sets his finely woven mysteries in Navajo country, wrote with more authority about the dilemma of Navajo tribal policemen faced with handling the bodies of anyone who has died, as the Navajo put it, "unprepared."

The ruins of the Wolf store, and others, at places like Canyon Diablo and Tolchaco, testify to the hardiness of the early Southwestern traders and their customers. Those early trading posts were contact points between the Indian and Anglo civilizations. Before the railroads, traders had to wagon-freight food and merchandise over hundreds of miles from established population centers in New Mexico. In turn, the traders shipped out their barter, the Indian arts, for eastern markets.

That started to change even before the arrival of the twentieth century. Railroads brought merchandise, and tourists, to the traders' doorsteps. Fred Harvey, as he built his series of hotels and restaurants along the Santa Fe route, almost immediately saw the commerciality of Indian art. Not long after the railroads came the automobile, and Harvey, from his hotels, sent out huge cars filled with tourists, on day trips to points of Southwestern interest, including trading posts.

Today some of the posts have evolved into a straight-through operation. No longer are they Indian-Anglo contact points, but agencies between Indian craftspeople and Anglo customers, both highly mobile. Tribal craftspeople earn a living selling their wares to trading posts like Hubbell's. The posts then sell the wares to visitors, either art collectors or pure tourists. These posts, which "do rugs," as Bill Malone said, have become the minority. The rest of the posts today are little more than convenience stores.

"There aren't really that many trading posts on the reservation any more that are really into crafts," said Malone. "It seems like the young people don't want to mess with it anymore. The posts get bought out by a Thriftway or a 7-11 outfit and revert back to doing just goods and gasoline. There are probably half a dozen posts that still do rugs."

Without the traders' early influence, there might not be any rugs to "do" today. Before 1900, Navajo weavers produced not rugs, but blankets, naturally worn by the Navajo as clothing. Then, in the 1890s, drought and overgrazing imperiled the tribe's indigenous economy. The traders suggested to the weavers that they could help themselves if they produced not blankets, but rugs. Not many rich Anglo customers would wear blankets to the office, but they would proudly array fine Navajo rugs in their homes. The traders offered better prices to weavers who brought in rugs, and soon the new industry was established. Some historians say the traders, with this act, saved the Navajo weavers' tradition. The traders also had a direct effect on the art, suggesting colors and designs for the rugs that they knew would appeal to the Anglo market. Hubbell, with watercolors, conceived and painted designs that he hung on his walls to inspire his weavers. In time, types of rugs became associated with the trading post where they were sold. Mobility today has diluted that association, when two weavers

123

from Cedar Ridge will drive three hours to get a fair price from Bill Malone.

The rugs at Hubbell's are beautiful, of course, but maybe even a stronger impression is of the timelessness of art. The work is skilled and meticulous and more than unhurried. It is not done in association with any sort of mechanical, artificial time. Instead, the reverse is true. The time as kept in a weaver's head is not measured in minutes or hours, but in the rhythm of warps and wefts. The Navajo does not weave a rug to fill time, but to create it. All Indian art, including ritual, is simply time being created. To the Anglo, the rugs represent this concept of time that is native to us all, and appealing because it is so peaceful. The rugs represent the harmony of natural time that is not accessible to persons on schedules. It is the kind of time kept by Spider Man and Spider Woman, who first taught the Navajos to weave, they say on looms that Spider Man built between the tall rock spires in Canyon de Chelly. Spider Man built the looms, and Spider Woman did the weaving. To this day, nature has never produced another weaver to equal her. Navajo parents from that time on have gathered samples of her craft to rub on the hands and arms of newborn girls, to ensure them skill, strength, and endurance. The weavers know that their strength is not theirs alone, but came from somewhere else.

"After they have made a few rugs, they need to have a kind of 'good-ways' ceremony, to keep things going well for them," said Malone. "It is a little blessing you go through with the medicine man. It's a private thing."

Bill Malone said maybe a thousand weavers bring their rugs to him. "I'll bet we probably do three thousand rugs a year here,"

124

he said. The rugs wait at Hubbell's in stacks around the room, in traditional styles identified by tags of authentication on which are also the weaver's name, her village, her photo, and the price. The rugs are not cheap. An average price for a 4-by-6 or 5-by-7 rug is fifteen hundred dollars. A 9-by-12 masterpiece, woven by Mae Begay of Pinon, listed for thirty-five thousand dollars. In Anglo terms, the rug took Begay a year to complete.

Malone still receives "scratch" rugs—the threads homespun from native wool—but commercial, prespun wool is in wide use. "A lot of weavers now are buying prespun wool, because it took longer to prepare the wool than it did to weave the rug," said Malone. "Until such time as the rug-buyer wants to pay twice as much for a rug that is hand-spun, over one that uses prespun wool, that's gonna be on the back burners.

"Oh, yes, you can tell the difference. Most of the prepared wool has already got the little ridges and knots out of it, so it makes a slicker looking rug," he said. "I've got a lot of hand-spun rugs, but most people will trip over them to get to the others."

The rugs move quickly, and constitute most of the post's business, followed, said Malone, by jewelry, baskets, and pottery. It wasn't long before Mae Begay's rug sold, to a couple from Chandler, Arizona.

"I think they are dairy farmers," said Malone. "They have the rug hanging on their dining room wall."

Did it sell for thirty-five thousand dollars?

"No," said Malone. "I think I sold it for about twenty."

That's why it is called a trading post.

Rug Room, Hubbell Trading Post National Historic Site, Arizona.

J. L. Hubbell ran his trading post at Ganado for fifty years, from 1880 to 1930, during which time he did much to point his Navajo customers and friends toward a sound economic footing. Hubbell knew what kind of Navajo goods would sell in the Eastern, Anglo market. He urged his weavers, who had been weaving handsome blankets for generations, to use heavier wool and to make rugs instead. With watercolors, he created designs he believed would sell, and urged the weavers to copy them. Hubbell's watercolor designs hang on the walls of the trading post today, and thousands of rugs are sold.

126

Freight wagon and hogan, Navajo Reservation, Arizona.

The Native American existence at the time of the trading posts centered on shelter, subsistence, trade, and water. The people lived in a harmony of spirit with land that anchored all their thoughts. Livestock, mostly sheep, constituted the main commerce. Wool was woven into blankets and rugs, or exchanged at trading posts for canned goods, clothing, tools, and wagons. Wagons gave the Navajos the mobility to haul goods and water across the vast expanse of their reservation. Pickup trucks and good paved highways streamline that operation today, and the shelters are less traditional.

Rock cabin, Vermillion Cliffs Wilderness Area, Arizona.

128

Juniper snag, Slickrock Canyon, Dolores River, Colorado.

Legends can be made, and mystical creatures born, in canyons where the rock is blue. For example: It was the time of colder days and golden leaves. Quietly the hunter followed his quarry into the canyon, hunger in his belly but doubt in his heart. He revered his fellowship with his brother the deer, and had prayed for the quick rebirth of the souls of many deer who had given up their lives in behalf of his. But this was a different matter. This deer was the most beautiful he had ever seen, the largest and the most graceful, with antlers that troubled the hunter. The huge rack turned gracefully up to the points, so many points that the hunter wondered if this might be the spirit father of all the deer. What would it mean, to kill him? He pressed on, then stopped, surprised, and looked around. He had reached the canyon's end, but where was the deer? He looked up the sheer, blue walls and felt fear. Then he saw it: the deer spirit had turned to wood and peered at him, safe and unafraid, from the rocks. The hunter was no longer afraid. He was relieved and honored to stand in the presence of what he now knew was the spirit father of all the deer. And he noticed that his hunger had disappeared.

Autumn leaves, Negro Bill Canyon Wilderness Area, Utah.

130

Plateau grasses in Arches National Park, Utah.

Evening primrose, Book Cliffs, Utah.

You are looking at countryside that produces some first-rate "new-age" cattle feed. The demand for corn-fed, heavily marbled prime-grade beef will always be with us, but the rising national health consciousness of the 1980s and 1990s created a market for a compromise between marbled beef and baked fish. People who worried about cholesterol but rolled their eyes at baked fish started asking for very lean beef at the supermarket. Lo and behold, the beef industry noticed. Beef now is available that is taken from lean animals, then infused with unsaturated vegetable oil for a marbling effect. Many of those lean animals are shipped from Southwestern plateau and desert rangeland.

Indian paintbrush in bloom, Colorado National Monument.

Southwestern wildflowers (and all the flowers are wild out here) in the act of fulfilling their color-intensity contracts with the stingy rainfall gods become vivid accent players in the continent's biggest rock garden. People who design and landscape rock gardens for a living might quibble with some of the placements, but those designers are like grammarians reading Shakespeare. Everyone else simply admires the arrangement, some to the point of organizing wildflower tours. Such tours in the Southwest can punctuate the calendar year-round. Desert residents, for example, mark their calendars for March, when the ocotillo, cholla, desert sage, and tiny desert daisy come into flower. About that same time, the lilac, in a good year, fills the foothills with its color and scent. At higher elevations, late spring brings the Indian paintbrush to life. In late summer the monsoon clouds float north from Mexico, wetting the desert and the plateau and bringing forth another generation of color.

Tansy aster, South Rim, the Grand Canyon.

134

Rainbow at sunset, Monitor and Merrimac, Utah.

The arch may be the most natural of all the combinations of strength and beauty. Certainly it is one of the most satisfying to the eye, and the most intriguing to the intellect. What holds it up? Any arch is a segment of a circle. The romantic notion is to believe that, anywhere an arch occurs, it is the earth's natural impulse to replicate itself. Human artist-romanticists hit on the keystone principle and achieved man-made arches. Cathedrals were the result. Keystones the size of sand grains or water molecules remain a natural triumph, which is probably for the best. Man-made rainbows soaring above parks of man-made arches would be very Mickey Mouse.

135

Delicate Arch and La Sal Mountains, Arches National Park, Utah.

White House Ruin, Canyon de Chelly, Arizona.

RITUALS: LIVING ANTIQUITY

Ed Dobson, an instructor of nonwestern art at a San Diego community college, owns his own Native American ritual site, a small canyon in the high desert of east central Arizona, near the New Mexico border. The canyon is held sacred by the Zuni Indian nation. "The canyon is extremely important to the Zunis," said Dobson. "It's their second-most-important shrine. It's part of their origin."

Ritual places are at the center of all Southwestern Indian cultures from the Anasazi on down. The Indian belief in oneness with the earth springs from such places, and the associated rituals embody the ancient mythology—probably the original mythology—of the harmony that was meant to exist between nature and humankind. The earth is the altar at which the Southwestern Indians lay their mortal and immortal souls.

Obviously Dobson's ownership of the canyon doesn't include spiritual rights. He feels more like the canyon's protector. He keeps the two hundred acres fenced, and the gate is secured with heavy chain and new padlocks. A key is kept in the Zuni tribal offices at the Zuni Pueblo in New Mexico, thirty miles east. Most modern Zunis have never visited the canyon, as most Christians have not visited Nazareth.

"The Zuni don't do rituals there any more, unfortunately," said Dobson. "Their interest in the canyon is mostly in a traditional, historical sense."

That tradition and history says the Zuni were wanderers, a people called teh ashiwi, descended from the Anasazi. They were searching for their homeland when they arrived at the canyon, which they called Hantlapinkia.

"The locals now call it Hardscrabble Canyon, and it is on Hardscrabble Wash," said Dobson, his voice lowering into story-telling gear. "But the Zuni called it Hantlapinkia. It is filled with wonderful petroglyphs. The Zuni were drawn to the canyon by their war gods. They received their war gods at the canyon. They had a battle with somebody, some other people there. They were joined by the 'bow priest,' which I think is their most important leader.

"From the canyon, they left, still looking for their homeland. They found it thirty miles east.'

Dobson has no idea when this might have happened. "There

is no time frame for this; this is mythology. The Zuni undoubtedly did come through there. They were probably migrating in from places like Chaco Canyon (in northwestern New Mexico) or places that had been abandoned. Supposedly they split into clans at the canyon. A group went south from there and was never heard from again. There is speculation that they might be the Aztecs. But that's pure speculation."

Knowing of these events brings a certain tentativeness to the step of a visitor, traveling alone and arriving at the canyon at midday. A dirt road leads off U.S. Highway 666, about midway between Sanders and St. Johns, makes a few turns through the scrubby juniper and high-desert growth, passes through Ed Dobson's heavily secured gate, and dwindles to tire tracks before disappearing on sandstone hardpan. The site is not so far off U.S. 666 that you could hear highway traffic, if there were any. There is a gentle rising and falling to the general flatness of the plateau, whose elevation here is around fifty-five hundred feet. "To the west, you can see forever," Dobson had said. It was good rangeland, but there was no recent sign of livestock—no animals at all, except for a couple of cottontails and the buzzing of a rattlesnake somewhere in the fractured sandstone. The human absence was distinct, though people had been here. In three places were signs of small campfires. Dobson has camped there, not alone. One night, he said, he heard a "spirit."

"One of those Zuni spirits is a figure called hututu. It makes a sound like somebody laughing. I heard that. Scared the hell out of me. It sounded like somebody making fun of me and laughing at me. I've heard owls out there, and it probably was an owl. But it didn't *sound* like an owl. I've heard owls, and they don't scare me."

The canyon was nearby, slashed suddenly into the sandstone, about fifty feet deep, growing wider from left to right and deeper in the same direction, curving out of sight around a bend to the west. (Around the bend, the canyon curves on, growing wider and deeper, for about a mile, until it ends in a cliff face.) It was very quiet.

I saw a faint trail along the bottom, maybe human, maybe not. The canyon sides were steep, and in places along the north rim sandstone slabs had collapsed into the canyon. The slabs offered no access. The only way into the canyon was down steps, carved into the rock long ago.

The steps were to the east, near the head of the canyon, in harder granite. The canyon toward the head narrowed into vertical, dark crevasses, becoming narrower until a man couldn't pass and wouldn't want to. The step-carvers' presence was overwhelming there.

Beyond and above the crevasses were deep, round potholes, churned out of the granite by ancient waters gathered by the shallow wash from terrain to the northwest. The upper chamber bored deep into the rock, and spun the current back up and over the chamber rim to another chamber below; waters twisted and blasted against the unyielding granite before escaping into the softer sandstone. These were the chambers where the war gods dwelled. There is now about them an abiding silence.

The teh ashiwi in their canyon rituals received their war gods. "Rituals re-create mythology," said Dobson. "At the canyon they would re-create the mythology of the war gods coming. There are those big, deep potholes, and there was foam and mist, and the war gods emerged from this foam."

Dobson bought the two-hundred-acre site in 1964 for ten thousand dollars. He had a degree in archaeology from the University of New Mexico and flew jets for the Air Force for five years. Then, at Arizona State University, he took a sculpture course that directed him into a career in nonwestern art.

By "nonwestern art," we mean ritual art, the art that humans have used to illustrate their mythology since the time of Zeus and Olympus. It is the art of the "spirit world," and it creates an interesting contradiction in terms. Americans take Indian art to be the very symbol of the West, when that art is not western at all.

At the same time, Americans are coming to understand the

difference. The failure of humanity to find salvation in the technological revolution has created a renewed awareness in our obligation to reside in harmony with nature. Ed Dobson put this awareness at the center of his spring 1991 class syllabus.

With 1991, the state of California was entering the hard-reality phase of a five-year drought. Measures were being passed requiring a thirty percent cut in water usage. When his spring semester class reported in late January of 1991, Dobson announced that the entire course would focus on preparing a series of rituals to bring rain.

"In California, a farmer will sit around and say, 'Oh, I wish it would rain,'" said Dobson. "A Zuni would never do that. A Zuni knows the spirit world would give rain."

He was not talking about the good old "rain dance," which Anglos have always characterized as Indians in loincloths and headdresses hopping in a circle. It was never as simple as that. It is an affront to the mythology to suppose that human harmony with earth is so selective that the rain god may be dialed up on some spiritual telephone. The Zunis in their rituals make no appeal. Their aim is to become one with the spirit of rain, the spirit of cloud, or the spirit that, in its time on earth, was a farmer. Who would be more sympathetic to the necessity for rain than the spirit of a farmer? To contact that spirit requires a person to leave this world, actually to cleanse himself of it, then embark on what the late Joseph Campbell called the "inward journey" to the spirit world. Rituals mark the steps in the transformation.

"The whole effort is to get into immediate contact with the elemental life of the cosmos, and to understand that it all lives," said Dobson. "Mountain life, cloud life, tree life: it's all alive. To get in contact with that power brings a dark sort of joy."

The poet D. H. Lawrence observed that joy when he came to live, and ultimately to stay and die, in New Mexico. When he watched the ritual of the deer dance, he saw that the dancers were not acting out deer roles. Instead, they "gently became" the deer.

Lawrence said he never truly understood religion until he came to New Mexico. Joseph Campbell, who probably should be called the father of the mythology revival, described rituals as "the literature of the spirit."

"When a dancer puts on a mask," said Dobson, "that spirit is there. It's not pretending. It is a soft, subtle 'being' of that spirit."

It is also very private. Most Native American cultures will let outsiders watch a few of their rituals, but not all. In one scene of the movie *Dances With Wolves* the buffalo have been away for a long time. A white hunter might say, "Oh, I wish the buffalo would come." But the Sioux embarked, with elaborate preparation, on a ritual sequence to bring the buffalo. Out on the plains, Kevin Costner saw the buffalo, a huge herd appearing from nowhere. He rode hard to tell the Sioux, rode right into the middle of their ritual, yelling, "Buffalo! Buffalo!" The Sioux, their sacred place violated, made to kill Costner before a shaman intervened.

The ritual of the hunt ensued. *Dances With Wolves* has been acclaimed as an accurate portrayal—as opposed to the endless stereotypes—of a Native American culture. The movie's hunt ritual goes beyond Native American accuracy, to the heart of the question of natural harmony. In this harmony, the hunter holds the quarry in sublime esteem. The animal dies, but the hunter takes pains to preserve and honor its spirit, so that it may return in another animal for another hunter. This is the cycle at the center of all mythology: life, death, ascension, and rebirth. In the movie a Sioux hunter eviscerated a fallen buffalo. He drank its blood and ate its flesh (apparently a testicle, but more traditionally the liver), taking prairie communion, and directing a momentarily reluctant Kevin Costner to do the same. At that holy, steaming altar, Costner knew better than to decline.

In recent Western history, that kind of commitment to harmony has at best been paid lip service. Ironically, it is now the cycle of the mythology itself that is being reborn. Mythology's

139

time has come again. Such stirrings are being felt not only by the techno-refugees, but also by keepers of the mythology, forced by legal eagles into battles on the plane of Western thought.

Not far south of Ed Dobson's canyon lies the Zuni people's most important shrine, a place that the Zunis call Kolhu/wala:wa. This is the where all Zunis go after death. At this place is a sacred lake, and residing beneath the lake are spirits called the Kokko. The lake is not far from the confluence of the Zuni and Little Colorado rivers, northwest of St. Johns. For centuries, every four years the Zunis have made a 110-mile pilgrimage from Zuni Pueblo to Kolhu/wala:wa, where they pray to the Kokko and to their ancestors for peace and harmony for the Zuni nation and for the entire world. The pilgrimage follows an ancient, sacred path called the Barefoot Trail, which in recent times has come into collision with hard, invisible lines put down by a surveyor's transit. Since 1985 the route to Kolhu/wala:wa has passed through a U.S. district court in Phoenix. In early 1990 a federal judge granted the Zunis easement rights across private land, every four years, at the time of the summer solstice, for up to sixty people on foot or on horseback, along an easement fifty feet wide. Testifying in the Zunis' behalf was former Arizona Senator and Secretary of the Interior Stewart Udall.

The Zunis also have moved to recover artifacts lost from their sacred sites, losses that began in the last century when anthropologists apparently made unauthorized visits to Kolhu/wala:wa and took religious objects. In this century many such objects, from many Native American cultures, have found their way into museums and private collections. Stories in *Zuni History*, a newspaper published by the tribal council, tell of the recovery, by mid-1991, of sixty-five "war god" figurines, called ahayu:da, from museums and collections in Maine, Oklahoma, Colorado, New York City, Wisconsin, New Mexico, Iowa, Canada, Pennsylvania, Missouri, and California.

The recovery effort began in 1978. In May 1991, Zuni councilman Joseph Dishta traveled to San Diego to take back an ahayu:da from the city's Museum of Man. The object, a wooden figurine, had been removed from the Zuni Reservation eighty years before by a motorcyclist who found it on a mountainside. The mountain in fact was a Zuni shrine.

"These items are considered sacred in the sense that they are protectors of Zuni land and the world as a whole," said Dishta. "They are looked upon as bringing prosperity for the people and the much-needed rain in the arid environment that we have in the Southwest."

On the day Dishta flew to San Diego to recover the object, the semiarid Southern California foothills were unusually lush with new growth. In early March, almost at the end of another dry, drought-deepening rainy season, it started to rain. One after another, the storms that for five years had stayed north of Southern California moved in from the Pacific with more rain. By the end of March almost seven inches had fallen on San Diego. It was the second-wettest March in San Diego since people started keeping records in 1867. In the media, the Western-world thinkers were calling it the Miracle of March. In Ed Dobson's lecture hall, students were looking over their shoulders.

Pueblo Bonito, Chaco Culture National Historic Park, New Mexico.

Aerial photography gives a better scope to the urban civilization achieved by the Anasazi at Chaco Canyon in northwestern New Mexico. Here is Pueblo Bonito, one of thirteen "grand houses" built in the narrow canyon after A.D. 900 by a people in transition from nomadism to agriculture. At its peak, around 1100, Pueblo Bonito stood four levels high, with six hundred rooms. The Anasazi built dams and canals to divert rainfall into their fields. Though the Spanish would not bring the horse and the wheel to the Southwest for another five hundred years, the Anasazi built a system of wide, straight roads to link the pueblos.

142

Cliff palace in winter, Mesa Verde National Park, Colorado.

Cowboy furniture, Cave Spring, Canyonlands National Park, Utah.

It was cowboys, out rounding up strays in southwestern Colorado on a bitter-cold winter day, who discovered the great pueblo at
Mesa Verde in 1888. The Anasazi had built the pueblo, Cliff Palace, beneath a huge, arched brow in the cliff face, which protected
the pueblo from wind and snow. What was good for one epoch was good for another. Cowboys working the ranges around
Canyonlands National Park, Utah, set up housekeeping in a natural room, away from the direct force of the elements.

Monty, Pack Creek Ranch, Utah.

144

Antique car and old cabin, Pack Creek Ranch, Utah.

Mormon settlers arrived in Utah in the 1800s and started ranches in the scenic, fertile, southern valleys. Later, Mormon colonies migrated into Arizona and began ranching operations there, above and below the Mogollon Rim, where they met up with other ranchers moving over from Texas. Ranching remains one of the Southwest's principal industries, and the cowboy is one of the Southwest's most vivid symbols. Extensive dude ranch opportunities await tenderfeet who want a taste of what it was like, though Monty, here, don't look like no dude.

The Redd Family, Dugout Ranch, near Canyonlands National Park, Utah.

Sometimes it is difficult to tell which is bigger, the myth or the reality. The myth has cowboys on horseback, each with a six-gun on his hip, a song on his lips, the lone prairie in his heart, and John Wayne in his blood. The reality has Matt, Heidi, and Adam Redd, leaning on a hitching post at Dugout Ranch, Utah, with the assembled tools for another day's work. It is work, these ranchers will tell you, that dwarfs the myth. Working a ranch under a Utah sky, in the shadow of red-rock spires, makes the movies look very flat and two-dimensional.

Horse and sheds, Dugout Ranch, Utah.

148

Pioneer cabin, Arches National Park, Utah.

Tools made such a difference. The Anasazi and other ancients built soaring apartments from rocks and sandstone, which yielded to the shaping blows of a blunt instrument. Such instruments were not suited to shaping logs from trees, though the Anasazi were creative enough to have thought of the idea. The people who came later continued to build rock houses, today of brick and cinder block, whose use is typical in Southwestern construction. Pioneers needing shelter, though, met their needs with the newfangled ax and bucksaw.

Hovenweep Castle, Hovenweep National Monument, southeastern Utah.

Yankee Boy Basin, San Juan Mountains, Colorado.

THE HIGH COUNTRY

Sunset, Great Sand Dunes National Monument, Colorado.

THE ARTISTS

In the twentieth century there has always been a market for Southwestern art, with its triumvirate powers of light, landform, and space working in synergy, the intensity of the whole surpassing the sum of the parts. But in the 1980s, the Santa Fe–Taos corridor became the third largest art market in the entire nation, with most of the total, naturally, being Southwestern art.

What is to account for the terrific national appeal of so regional an art? Organization has played a part. Since the 1960s, the Cowboy Artists of America (CAA) and the National Academy of Western Art (NAWA) have promoted Western and Southwestern art by providing venues for education, competition, exhibitions, and shows.

Of course, the artists' skills have much to do with the art's appeal. The application of those skills has become steadily more competitive not only through the CAA and NAWA, but also as artists from everywhere continue to relocate to the Southwest. If Southwestern images appeal so strongly to the general public, imagine their pull on an artist. Santa Fe hotel directories in 1991 listed 133 galleries doing business in the Santa Fe–Taos corridor.

More art, and better art, continues to become available.

But with a few exceptions—Hurd, O'Keeffe, Boren, Marks, Naegle, Parrish, Rippel, and some others—patrons don't buy the artist. They buy the picture. What draws them is not a familiar name, but a compelling place—or the picture of that place—where light, landform, and space come together in a way that touches some fundamental awareness in all people.

Since the elements predate the awareness, the mystery must abide with the elements. Artists and patrons alike are regularly heard to say there is something "magical" about the Southwest. I believe the magic has to do with the clarity of the three elements—nowhere else are they on such plain view. Visitors in the Southwest (and all humans are visitors in the Southwest, whether they remain five days or fifty years) can believe they are looking at the planet as it was a billion years ago. Thus the Southwest has the curious feel of being a "new" planet, where human visitors have just arrived. The illusion is created by the clarity of light, landform, and space. The visitor, waking up in a hotel room or opening a studio, may be stirred as if seeing this clarity for the first time. It is a daily ritual of discovery.

153

Indian symbol above right; rainbow.

It was from room 525 in La Fonda Hotel, for example, that I saw Southwestern light as if for the first time. The bells of St. Francis Cathedral had issued their 6 A.M. wake-up call, not a tolling of bells at so delicate an hour, but a contrapuntal texture that filled in spaces in the silence. The north-facing windows of room 525 gave a westerly view across a shallow valley, cobbled in the corals and greens of downtown Santa Fe, toward the pink distance beyond.

At that hour in June, dawn was already well under way. From the window I could look east to the cathedral across the street. To my eyes it stood dark, almost in silhouette, because the sun was just rising over a ridge in the middle distance directly behind the cathedral. This particular sunrise was framed exactly between the bell towers, and suddenly brightness streamed around the sides of the cross atop the clerestory's facade. The sunlight followed the bell music across the valley, filling in spaces in the darkness. Never had I seen quite so close a collaboration between sound and light.

The sunlight slid down the walls of the hotel and reached our window. I thought of how at dawn sunlight melts downward, over mountains and walls; at sunset, sunlight rises, with the darkness right behind it, until only the mountain tips stand briefly pink above the gray ocean of night. At dawn, the shadows seem less to arrive upon a wall than to gradually to emerge from it, like pictures developing on photographic paper. At dusk, the shadows recede into the wall, growing ever fainter like the fading illumination of a candle about to go out. At dusk all the patterns seem to return to where they came from, until no distinctions remain and the bare wall glows with twilight.

The white plaster walls in room 525 were pearl-blue with the progressing dawn. Then the first sunlight peeked under the window's brow. From the wall, a square of gold rose to meet it. The sunlight lit up the wall like a match touched to a lantern; the process was not transition but ignition. The gold square gave way at once to a brilliant white light, too bright to be assigned a shape.

Yet it was not blinding. I watched the light gather intensity until the wall seemed to vibrate under its power. The intensity spent itself in a moment, and then the light spread out. It reminded me of adjusting the mantle in the lantern. The shadow of the window frame appeared. It was a very dark, very stark, shadow, characteristic of shadows in Santa Fe, because of the clarity of the light there.

Why the light is so clear has never been exactly explained. Physicists, if they brought their instruments to bear, might provide some scientific answers. Power is obviously involved. Southwestern light is like a top-quality stereo system, having great power at its disposal; if you turn it up all the way, you could hear it in Kansas City. The legitimate value of all that power is the clarity it brings to music played at everyday ranges. Southwestern light imparts that same clarity to everyday vision. At full power, it can ignite the dawn. In its everyday ranges, it shows objects with their edges clean, all their nuances of color and tone intact.

The physicists, preoccupied with fission and fusion and such, have not been much interested. Most of what we know about New Mexico light has been explained by artists, among whom the subject is a passion. I might add writers to that group, though we suffer the constraint of not working directly with the medium. Essayist E. B. White said that a writer's medium is sound: a writer's style is the sound his words make on paper. The artist's medium is light: an artist's style is the light his or her strokes make on canvas, or the light the fingers make on clay, or the light the shutter transmits to film.

Being a writer and a native Texan, I have devoted considerable effort to producing the sound of light on paper. It has been the sound of Texas light, in the main, and I cannot claim to have achieved definitive results. In the end, however, all of my contemplations arrive back at the same place—at a strong suspicion that Texas light is horizontal, that its principal property is distance. Texas light tends to overcome horizons.

My strong suspicion about Southwestern light is that it is vertical, and that its principal property is levitation. Southwestern light tends to cancel gravity. Such light appears fragile, like a ballerina. But like the ballerina, Southwestern light possesses tremendous power: the power to suspend gravity.

That suspension runs through the body of Southwestern art, becomes its subordinate theme. Only the weight of a frame keeps the best examples hanging on the gallery walls. An interesting number of artists choose subjects of intense plainness—doors, skulls, and garden gates come to mind—as if to remove all other distractions from their investigation of the properties of Southwestern light.

Such pure studies make interesting science, and wonderful art, with the contemplative magnetism of a kachina doll or a Zuni chant. Levitating single objects, however, is only a side effect of light's power to cancel gravity beneath whole landscapes. When the mountains and mesas in a painting appear to belong equally to earth and sky, you have the big picture of Southwestern light at work.

The role of the landform in the partnership is spectacular and distinctive. New Mexico, for example, appears put there by a stamp that God made long ago, incorporating the signature mesas, mounts, buttes, and arroyos within precise boundaries and pressing them into the warm earth dough. The effect today is that when you cross those boundaries from Texas or Arizona, inside half a mile you find yourself suddenly, distinctively, in New Mexico. The reds of ancient oxides rise from the slashed earth to change the blue of the sky, and the sky in turn changes the color and texture of the earth minute by minute from daybreak until dark. Southwestern days become a gallery of glimpses, showing improbably beautiful landscapes made impossibly so, the picture changing with the light all day long. People have long felt compelled to come and tour this magical world, and artists have always been among them. Today artists take sketchbook and color case

and camera, and prowl the landscapes in utility vehicles, never knowing what they might see, even in places where they have looked before.

The tableaux are emotional, with not much possibility of cool response. Albuquerque artist Morris Rippel, who also had a career as a licensed architect, has produced Southwestern scenes noted for their reason and realism. Rippel says he never painted to evoke any particular emotions. When he paints, he says, he is "documenting." The results, of course, are a vivid accounting of emotions occurring naturally in the Southwestern landscape.

You can't look at as straightforward a work as *Saddle Rock*, a watercolor of a high desert red-rock outcropping by the late Wyoming artist Stephen Naegle, and not feel involvement.

Artists of the realistic school might weep with joy on arriving in the Southwest. Impressionists are seen to grin a lot as well. It was another kind of extraordinary light—Paris light and French countryside light—beneath which the original Impressionist masters—Cezanne, Renoir, van Gogh, Monet, Pissarro—conducted their investigations. Their results, vibrating with color and powerful with suggestion, provided a superior model for artists drawn to the Southwest by the mysteries of the light. So direct is the Impressionists' influence, on occasion, that you can visit the galleries and stroll past the swirling, broad-brushed landscapes and think you are looking at van Gogh by Joe Blogh.

In their middle ground, Southwestern artists may place subjects drawn from three cultures. Native Americans have inhabited the Southwest for a thousand years. Starting in the 1500s, the Spanish established a presence in the area that has continued to this day. Spaniards founded the town of Santa Fe in 1609 as the capital of the New Mexico province. And the Anglo-Europeans began arriving in the nineteenth century. Anglo artists were gathering in the area by the turn of the twentieth century; in 1915, six artists founded the Taos Society of Artists.

Art and architecture were routine activities in each of the

155

three cultures. The result of that activity—pottery, baskets, blankets, ritual kachina dolls, jewelry, sculpture, furniture—constitutes a body of native Southwestern art very much in demand today. The result for modern Southwestern art may be a painting like Howard Terpning's *Preparing for the Sundance*, which shows Indian shamans preparing a ritual dancer in elaborate body paint and garlands. The work presents a striking, multicultural painting within a painting. Albuquerque artist Wilson Hurley, noted for his Grand Canyon scenes, produced a three-canvas study of Anasazi ruins built into the cliff faces at Canyon de Chelly that shows the virtual oneness of the Anasazi culture with the landscape.

The Spanish culture provides subjects like mission chapels and village scenes as well as historical depictions of the early explorations and, later, ranch and presidio life. The Anglos' arrival shows up in paintings of trappers, mountain men, miners, cavalry soldiers, and, of course, cowboys. Cowboys, horses, and livestock are everywhere in Southwestern art.

Whatever these pictures may be about, their common theme is space. Everything happens outdoors. The presence of Southwest space is so strong that we find a village street scene confining—maybe comfortably so, but it still seems an interior that can be exited. And beyond that exit is, well, grandeur: eternal, irrepressible grandeur that even the dullest human intellect is powerless to resist.

That may be the principal secret of Southwestern art's appeal: light, landform, and space presenting a natural grandeur with which all human beings identify. We have been conditioned to do so since the time of the caves. Human beings, as much as wolves and eagles, first thrived on earth as creatures of the outdoors. In our genetic material we still carry those stamps—mythologist Joseph Campbell called them "memories carried on the nerves"—that call even the most urban-dependent Manhattanite to an occasional stroll in the park. This was the original love-hate relationship. We strove to escape the dangers and the hardships of

nature while constantly being pulled back by her beauty.

With the beginning of the 1990s, it became clear that nature was calling to humankind in a new and special way. Through the millennia, humans had been wandering the planet in search of deliverance from want, a place of safety, comfort, self-preservation, and, ultimately, immortality. All human advances were based on that instinctive drive. Since the 1700s, those advances have been mainly industrial. In the 1900s, they became scientific and then technological. Now we are almost to the twenty-first century, riding a planet riddled with blight, and people are seeing that technology will not save them. They begin to understand that salvation rests not with their defeat of nature, but in their collaboration with it. That is the only answer, and in arriving at it, humankind comes full circle.

The technogeneration thus becomes keenly interested in the ways of the American Indian, keeper of the principal North American mythology that describes the harmony in which humans and nature are meant to exist. In San Diego in the summer of 1991, Indian leaders, artists, writers, and educators met to consult with planners of the new National Museum of the American Indian, due for completion in 1998 as part of the Smithsonian Institution complex in Washington, D.C. Museum director and Indian attorney W. Richard West, Jr., said contemporary interest in Indian culture "surpasses anything I have known most of my life. What you see at the present time is a flowering of Indian culture that I find positively profound." Writer, painter, professor, and Pulitzer Prize winner N. Scott Momaday of the University of Arizona said of the museum, "We must organize it in a way to call attention to the Native American connection to nature."

A connection to nature is the very theme of Southwestern art. Wherever Americans, whatever their background, feel compelled toward this new, yet very old, rapport, they will find pleasure in taking home an idea of what nature always looked like.

Emmi Whitehorse, painter, Santa Fe, New Mexico.

Santa Fe artist Emmi Whitehorse, a Navajo, with her painting that echoes the creations of her
ancestors, who left pictographs across the Southwest as a record of life in their time. Southwestern art
finds much of its inspiration in history and place and people. The Whitehorse painting, evoking all
three, suggests the Native American belief, rising in antiquity and continuing today, that harmony
between people and place is the fount of all history, and the force that drives all life.

158

Sunset, Sandia Crest, Cibola National Forest, New Mexico.

Many artists came to the Southwest from somewhere else. Among those are artists who didn't intend to stop there, but were just passing through on their way to somewhere else. Then, as they typically describe it, they saw something or felt something in the Southwestern light, and slammed on the brakes. They never left again. Artists don't relocate to the Southwest to paint seascapes. They arrive eager to paint the Southwest, or the extraordinary effect that the Southwest appears to have on ordinary things, such as rock faces and dead trees.

Dead trees after winter storm, near Durango, Colorado.

160

Traditional pueblo near Taos, Sangre de Christo Mountains, New Mexico.

Indian merchant on the plaza, Santa Fe, New Mexico, and oven and steps, Taos Pueblo, New Mexico.

Though by no means complete, the communications revolution has reached all the country's corners, linking people of all backgrounds into a common information system. At any given hour, all of the people can be on the same page. Residents of Taos, of Boise, of Casa Grande, of Baton Rouge, of Bangor, and of Tallahassee can all watch the same person emoting over the same bowl of breakfast flakes at the same time. People in Taos can be as familiar with "good cholesterol" and Michael Jackson as people in Los Angeles and New York. Some loss of regionality occurs when the news, products, and future sound the same all across the country. But people are still free to make decisions. They may decide that bread baked the old way is still worth it. Their view of reality may make more sense than the opinions from New York and California, and part of their vision may be that you can't improve on turquoise as the color for window trim.

162

Ladder and lilac door, Taos Pueblo, New Mexico.

Blanket on pueblo wall, Taos Pueblo, New Mexico.

163

It's a chicken-egg question: which came first, the artist, or the pueblo? It was important to somebody that that door be lilac, and equally important to others that their doorways be teal. Color and design are passions that run like hawsers back through the generations of the Southwestern cultures, to the time of the intricate patterns on Anasazi pottery. The Anasazi, believing they came from the earth, saw what a vivid earth it was beneath the blue, blue sky. They might have easily conceived the notion that color was a living expression of harmony. The landscape had a similar effect on artists arriving much, much later, some of them who came only to visit, but, through some harmonious bonding of their own with the place, found it impossible to leave. Invariably, in explaining that decision, they talk about color and the way color vibrates in the Southwest.

164

Chapel at San Miguel, Santa Fe, New Mexico.

165

Window detail, Chapel San Miguel, Santa Fe, New Mexico, and church in Golden, in Ortiz Mountains, New Mexico.

Franciscan friars started putting up the adobe walls of the San Miguel Chapel in 1610, the year after Governor Don Pedro de Peralta's decision to place the capital of the new Mexican province at Santa Fe. Today, Santa Fe is the oldest continuous seat of government in the United States, and the San Miguel Chapel, three blocks east of Santa Fe's central plaza, is among the nation's oldest churches. The friars spread out from Santa Fe to "civilize" the natives and bring them to Christianity. Other missions were built, among them a church that still stands with the bell in its tower, in the ghost town of Golden, near Santa Fe. The Pueblo Rebellion drove the Spanish from the Santa Fe area in 1680, and records of the church were burned. But when the Spanish returned twelve years later, the church was intact. Visitors find that exterior buttresses have been added, to take strain off the 400-year-old walls.

166

Rock pinnacle, Snowmass Wilderness Area, Colorado.

Rainbow over the Maroon Bells, Snowmass Wilderness Area, Colorado.

Author D. H. Lawrence, whose final resting place is in the mountains northeast of Taos, said the southern Rocky Mountains were the most beautiful he had ever seen. From the New Mexico Plateau, the Rockies emerge as two ranges—the San Juans on the west and the Sangre de Cristos to the east. The ranges flank the Rio Grande as they climb north into Colorado. The Continental Divide touches both ranges, looping from the Sangre de Cristos to the San Juans and back again, on its way north. The terrain climbs rapidly into true alpine mountains, where the clarity of vision, typical of higher elevations like the Maroon Bells, puts every detail of earth and sky within reach of the poet's understanding.

Inn at Santa Fe, Santa Fe, New Mexico.

HARVEY GIRLS

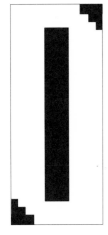n 1945 Metro-Goldwyn-Mayer released *The Harvey Girls*, a movie starring Judy Garland, John Hodiak, Ray Bolger, and, if you can believe this, Angela Lansbury as a dance hall floozy.

The movie said a lot about the Southwest of the late nineteenth and early twentieth centuries. During that time the Southwest was being opened up to the Anglo trade. Some pictures coming out of the Southwest at that time were accurate, and some were less than that, factual at one extreme and fantasized at the other. *The Harvey Girls* manages to combine the extremes.

The movie was about the collaboration between the Atchison, Topeka and Santa Fe Railway and the Fred Harvey Company. Rail travel had revolutionized transportation across the West after the Civil War. The first transcontinental link was completed at Promontory, Utah, in 1869, where the Union Pacific and Central Pacific companies met to drive the golden spike. The Atchison, Topeka and Santa Fe in the 1870s completed a route from Chicago across the Southwest to Los Angeles. The rails entered New Mexico at the northeast corner, dipped south of Santa Fe to Albuquerque, then cut west to Gallup, Holbrook, Winslow, Flagstaff,

and Kingman, entering California at Needles. The trains were dirty, smoky, not particularly comfortable, and very hot in summertime. But they beat the pants off horseback and stagecoaches, particularly over distances, and they could carry a lot more passengers.

Travel was basic in the early days. The seats were hard. Trains didn't have dining cars or anything you might call indoor plumbing. When passengers were hungry, they waited until the train reached a town, jumped off, and found what they could to eat before the train departed again twenty minutes later. The food quality was not very good, and vendors were not above gouging the captive clientele.

Fred Harvey was an Englishman, an entrepreneur with style, and the conditions of rail travel in the Southwest caught his attention. He proposed to the Santa Fe that he set up a series of restaurants and hotels along the railway line to give passengers good food, reasonable prices, consistent service, and some creature comforts. The Santa Fe managers liked the idea. In 1876 Harvey and Santa Fe entered into an agreement: the railroad would construct and own the restaurant and hotel buildings, and Harvey

169

Indian symbol above right; lizard.

would run them. Santa Fe justified the construction expense by reasoning that the promise of good meals and overnight accommodations along the way would attract more passengers. Harvey, meanwhile, would realize the revenues of the food and hotel service. Harvey set to work from headquarters in Santa Fe's Union Station in Kansas City.

The establishments became known as Harvey Houses. Fred Harvey didn't do things halfway. The restaurants were set with linen, silver, and china. Service was professional. Harvey managers hired and trained the waitresses that became the famous Harvey Girls, in their long black dresses and starched, spotless white aprons. The Harvey credo was "The trains must be fed." Arriving trains signaled ahead the number of passengers wanting a meal, and when the passengers detrained and entered the restaurant, the food was ready. Kansas City steak dinners became the Harvey House trademark. The entire service was ruled by efficiency. Harvey's intention was to afford travelers good food in comfortable, unhurried surroundings, yet have them back on the train in thirty minutes. At Fred Harvey's lead, Harvey Houses also acquired a reputation for civility, an influence that became felt in the Southwestern towns beyond the grounds of the Harvey establishments.

MGM's movie portrayed all this, down to the gong that was sounded when passengers arrived, signaling the girls to begin serving. But it cast Judy Garland as a mail-order bride, coming from Ohio to marry a rancher. On the train also are Harvey Girls, coming to open a restaurant at "Sandrock," a fictional but wily name for a Southwestern town surrounded by a landscape shaped and colored by the sedimentary rock of ancient seabeds.

The Harvey Girls and Judy Garland arrive in Sandrock at the end of roughly a twelve-hundred-mile train trip from Kansas City, stepping off the train as fresh and crisp in their big dresses as if they had just come from the boudoir. Sandrock's main street, meanwhile, is awash with young men, wearing bright western shirts and jeans, who all can sing and dance. A big production

number ensues, with Judy leading the ensemble in Johnny Mercer's "The Atchison, Topeka and the Santa Fe." A few Indians stand around, looking positively ornamental. Across the way is the decadent Alhambra, a saloon and dance hall run by John Hodiak in a Black Bart moustache that barely hides the streak of gold in his heart. Angela Lansbury does a can-can in black bustier and orange boa. At midday the Alhambra is clogged with whooping customers, maybe a couple hundred of them, whose jobs, apparently, will wait. The town judge and Hodiak are in cahoots. The suggestion is that the Harvey House is going to civilize the town and put the Alhambra out of business. The judge is worried about that; next thing, he tells Hodiak, the townspeople will want to start up the church again.

Judy Garland's rancher turns out to be Chill Wills, who plays the country galoot to the hilt. They are mutually appalled, he by her gentility, she by his galootedness, and within minutes they call the whole thing off. She goes off to become a Harvey Girl and ....

Well, it was just a musical. Today we would call it a parody. But in 1945 men, women, and children who knew very little about the Southwest went to the movies in places like Cleveland and Mobile, paid their nickels, and received some definite signals about life in the Great Southwest, where the ranchers were ignoramuses, the judge was on the take, half the citizens immigrated from Radio City Music Hall, and the rest of them were drunks or thieves. *The Harvey Girls* got mixed reviews. Said critic Richard Winnington: "Anybody who did anything at all in America up to 1900 is liable to be made into a film by MGM." Said the *New York Herald Tribune*'s critic: "A perfect example of what Hollywood can do with its vast resources when it wants to be really showy."

If *The Harvey Girls* revealed any real information about Southwestern life, it remained secondary with the critics. It proves the power of stereotypes that Hollywood could find the Southwest such a fertile filming ground, and tell so little about it. Hollywood literature made little provision for ordinary life in the Southwest, or for cultural history, or for the presence, as real people, of the Southwestern natives, unless confrontation were involved. Hollywood was always big on confrontation. Americans received a tilted picture of the Southwest as a place not of cowboys, or of Indians, but of cowboys and Indians. The Southwest appeared to be a place where there was always winning to be done, and the good guys always did it.

In real life, Fred Harvey and the railway paid close attention to details of Southwestern culture, and ultimately became its national purveyors. In the early days the company concentrated on its mission to feed the trains. At the turn of the century, the Harvey Company, with the Santa Fe's concurrence, decided the buildings that housed the restaurants and hotels should reflect the culture of the region they served. Harvey architects worked under the commission to design buildings that were reconstructions—or, more precisely, reconceptions—of historical or indigenous architecture. The result was that some Harvey Houses reflected the Spanish style, others echoed Indian pueblo construction, and one—the old Alvarado Hotel at Albuquerque—paid respects to the missions of California, at the end of the line.

The Alvarado has been torn down. But if you have visited the Grand Canyon and climbed the Watchtower or stayed in Bright Angel Lodge, you have seen examples of buildings designed and constructed by the Harvey Company and the Santa Fe Railway.

Harvey's chief architect, designer, and decorator was Mary Colter, who in forty-six years with the Harvey Company designed or contributed to the design of seventeen buildings along the Santa Fe right-of-way in New Mexico and Arizona. Among them were Bright Angel Lodge, Hopi House, Phantom Ranch, and the Watchtower at the Grand Canyon; La Posada at Winslow; El Navajo at Gallup; El Ortiz at Lamy, south of Santa Fe; and in Santa Fe the interior of La Fonda Hotel. The Bright Angel Lodge picked up on the motif of the thunderbird, the Indian symbol for

"the powers of the air." The Watchtower was inspired by tower ruins found among the pueblos at Mesa Verde and Canyon de Chelly. La Posada revived the spirit of the old ranchos of the Spanish dons, and El Navajo was a modern interpretation of traditional Indian themes. These facades and designs, with the help of Santa Fe advertising, came to be synonymous in the national mind with the shape and spirit of the Southwest.

Colter also designed and oversaw the construction of museums for Indian art, and shops in which the Harvey Company sold Indian art, jewelry, pottery, and blankets. Harvey thus carried a giant step farther the Indians' natural practice of congregating wherever the trains stopped and showing their wares alongside the tracks.

Though the Harvey Company's main interest was in "feeding the trains," in the early 1900s it began to consider the possibility of providing an automobile touring service. The company was convinced that the Southwest itself was becoming a destination. Tourists drawn by the promise of Southwestern vistas and pueblo sites would travel by train to Harvey hotels, then take day trips in the huge, new, touring cars provided by Harvey. The company called the trips Indian Tours and saw much potential in the use of the automobile.

What the company had seen was the beginning of the end. Auto travel in the Southwest had been nonexistent before the turn of the century, and it remained insignificant, in terms of long-distance travel, into the 1920s. Then as cars became bigger, faster, more comfortable, and more reliable, Americans began to demand a good system of roads to drive them on. By the 1930s, construction was under way on a national system of paved highways. Highway 66, the principal auto route from Chicago to Los Angeles, ironically paralleled almost exactly the Santa Fe tracks across the Southwest. Auto travel, once it became practical, gave tourists a freedom of mobility that was hard to ignore.

Santa Fe countered with luxury rail travel. The railway began

171

pulling passenger trains with beautiful new diesel engines whose orange-and-silver "warbonnet" livery became an instant classic. The sight of these engines pulling their silver trains through the wide-open spaces became one of the strongest images of the twentieth-century Southwest. The company instituted Super Chief service, exclusively first class on completely air-conditioned trains, from Chicago to Los Angeles in the late 1930s, with the Harvey Company in charge of the dining and lounge cars. This kind of travel appealed to movie stars, whose appearance at stations and Harvey Houses along the way attracted crowds from the towns.

Then World War II began, and with it the end of any form of tourism for a while. Santa Fe and Harvey were busy transporting and feeding troops for the war's duration. After the war, with good highways in place and better ones on the way, and transcontinental air travel a reality, rail passenger traffic spiraled downward. Traveler services and amenities shifted to motels and restaurants that lined the highways in a blaze of neon. Santa Fe began closing or selling the facilities it had built for the Harvey Company. With such decisions, the buildings immediately became part and parcel of Southwestern history, deserving of preservation. When Santa Fe closed La Posada at Winslow in 1957, it was national news. That same year, El Navajo at Gallup was demolished.

Santa Fe kept La Posada intact, using part of it for offices and part of it as a dormitory for Amtrak train crews. For a building in a land where pueblo ruins date back a thousand years or more, La Posada had acquired amazing historical significance in barely sixty years. On June 19, 1991, Flagstaff's newspaper, the *Arizona Daily Sun*, published an editorial identifying La Posada as "one of northern Arizona's most historic buildings," and gently urging the city of Winslow ("we do not wish to tell the people of Winslow how to conduct business") to spend the money for its restoration. The editorial said the railway was interested in leasing the building to city government on a long-term basis. Winslow should respond, said the paper, and make La Posada "a civic center really worth talking about." Winslow, the paper reported, had commissioned a feasibility study, fearful that grand old La Posada could become a white elephant.

The Fred Harvey Company has long since run out of trains to feed, but it still maintains a strong presence in the Southwest, particularly at the Grand Canyon. The company also, I discovered, operates concessions at some of the national parks. I was leaving the visitor center at the Petrified Forest National Park when I spotted the familiar Harvey logo inviting visitors into the snack bar.

A snack bar was what it was—a counter and trays and tables, with no elegance in sight among the chrome and Formica and racks of chips. And at that hour, late in the day, the place was deserted. But the old Harvey spirit was intact. The snack bar is approached along a corridor, and the instant I poked my head beyond the end of the corridor, a friendly voice called to me from behind the counter, a good fifty feet away: "Evening, sir, can I help you with anything?" I could see the founder smiling.

Santa Fe caboose.

Modern railroad technology has rendered cabooses obsolete, but the long freights cruising at ninety miles per hour across the Arizona plateau still look tailless without them. For a century the red cabooses of the Atchison, Topeka and Santa Fe Railway were moving trademarks of Southwestern life. Now they are museum objects, as are the grand old Santa Fe depots, such as La Posada at Winslow, in whose vaulted corridors and manicured courtyards passengers once strolled while waiting for the train. Winslow civic leaders in the l990s were hoping to spare La Posada from the fate of Alvarado, the Albuquerque depot that was torn down.

174

Though the snow never disappears at these elevations, below the treeline the Rockies and San Juans and Sangre de Cristos come alive with color in summertime. People who come to the Rockies in winter to ski can return in summer to roll in the mountain clover. Pictured here are the San Juans in June and July, in the Uncompahgre National Forest, which angles across southwestern Colorado from below Grand Junction to Telluride. In this area north of Telluride, Mount Sneffels is the highest peak, at 14,150 feet. This is the season that draws visitors to the colorful old mining districts from Durango up to Telluride, Silverton, and Ouray, and over to Creede, with all the floral scenery in between an added bonus. Or maybe it's the other way around.

Mountain wildflowers, San Juan Mountains, near Telluride, Colorado.

High pasture, Sneffels Range, San Juan Mountains, Colorado.

176

Durango and Silverton narrow-gauge railroad .

177

Elks Lodge, Ouray, Colorado and deserted cabin, ghost town of Alta, San Juan Mountains, Colorado.

The discovery of gold in Colorado in the mid-nineteenth century brought prospectors roaming through the Rocky Mountains, battling the rock and the elements in a search for riches that in reality has not ended yet. Evidences of the prospectors' efforts still dot the mountain slopes. There was, in fact, gold and silver, and plenty of both; around the biggest claims, towns grew and prospered. Then the boom passed. Some mines still conceal wealth, silver particularly, but prices don't justify bringing it out. But the towns thrived again by capitalizing on their colorful history. The Durango and Silverton narrow-gauge railroad, operating on tracks over which ore cars once moved, carries visitors on a scenic trek along the Animas River to mining towns carefully restored to their Victorian heydays.

178

Falls through travertine, Jemez Creek, Santa Fe National Forest, New Mexico.

Waterfall in Yankee Boy Basin, San Juan Mountains, Colorado.

The image of the wilderness is one of silence, of a place where one goes to escape the rattle and hum of civilized life. But silence is the same elusive visitor here, because there is a civilization of the land that cloaks the wilderness with rhythms and natural songs that have no verses, no refrain, no beginning, and no end. A visitor may come to a stream at any hour of the day, or a corresponding hour of night, and know that he will encounter a song of life that has been sung at that place for a million years. The effect on the listener is one of reassurance, of the knowledge that he is not alone.

179

180

Aspen along Henson Creek, Uncompahgre National Forest, Colorado.

The most widely known, and arguably the most beautiful, sight in a region of beautiful sights is the aspen in fall, when they start to turn. When their leaves shimmer in the breeze, the aspen stands become golden ponds in the evergreen forest. Wherever in the world Colorado is mentioned, pictures of mountains and snow and golden aspen cross the mind's eye. They may be a cliche, but no one is ever heard to complain.

181

Aspen turning, Rio Grande National Forest, Colorado.

182

Victorian house, Telluride, Colorado.

Frosted trees, San Miguel Canyon, and Telluride sunset, Colorado.

Telluride is an old mining town that has become one of the most alluring stops, winter or summer, on the visitors' circuit, though reaching the town requires a roundabout trip of about forty miles from U.S. Highway 550. Restored gingerbread Victorian houses line the residential streets in the Historic District, while downtown offers accommodations, restaurants, and shops. Major skiing areas are nearby. This November storm dropped a foot of snow.

Winter scene, San Miguel Range, Uncompahgre National Forest, Colorado.

LOOKING BACK TO THE FUTURE

In the 1940s, engineers in communications centers in New York and Los Angeles took up positions behind banks of control consoles and started a revolution. It was slow, and it was bloodless, but the revolution begun by those early engineers absolutely changed the way Americans thought and bought and talked.

The engineers did their work with audio and video signals. The medium was television. At first the engineers could send their signals only through transmitters with limited range. Before 1946 all television reception was local, and exclusive to big cities such as New York, Boston, and Pittsburgh. In 1945 there were nine television stations on the air in the United States.

Then, in 1946, the engineers figured out a way to send their signals through a cable. They called it a coaxial cable, and they laid such cables between New York, Philadelphia, Boston, and Washington. By 1948 cable had been extended into the Midwest, so that stations "on the cable," as they said, in the East and Midwest could receive network shows simultaneously. In 1951 a microwave link was established to the West Coast. Suddenly national television transmission was possible. By 1950 there were

ninety-seven stations on the air nationally. In 1951, ninety-four of them carried President Truman's address to the San Francisco peace conference that drew up the treaty officially ending World War II in the Pacific.

In Arizona and New Mexico, as dawn broke the chill over the Southwest and brought color to the vast, purple land, Southwesterners would sit down with their newspapers, the *Arizona Republic* and the *Albuquerque Journal*, and read about these developments as if they were reports from another planet. Remarkably, they were reports from one lifetime. Most of today's leaders in Southwestern government and business were nine or ten years old at that time.

The early morning was cool over the Southwest, and clear, and quiet—whether you listened to it from your window or through your radio. There were a few AM radio stations, some police and railroad shortwave traffic, and signals to guide the commercial airliners—DC-3s hopping from Albuquerque to Phoenix at seven thousand feet on their way to Los Angeles. Otherwise, the Southwestern airspace was calm. But there developed in the Southwesterners a sense of waiting, and of curious excitement, because this thing called television was obviously headed their way. By 1955, four years after completion of the transcontinental link, the nation had 439 television stations. In 1953, Albuquerque's first television station, KOAT, went on the air. The first Phoenix telecast, from station KPHO, was seen in 1949.

Thus were sown the revolution's seeds. Though stations in Albuquerque and Las Cruces and Phoenix and Tucson could receive national programs on the cable-microwave system, they still could transmit only locally, and be received only by antenna-equipped homes and sets within range of their transmitters. People too far beyond the cities' fringes were left in the dark. Even in the cities, television remained a curiosity, an entertainment, though the Canadian social analyst Marshal McLuhan was already saying that the medium would become the message and create a global village.

In the late 1970s and 1980s the engineers perfected a system of transmitting television signals via satellites to local cable companies that provided cable service straight into the living room. Suddenly, instead of three or four local channels (Albuquerque by the 1990s had six), viewers had access to forty channels, or fifty or sixty. These viewers were not only in the big cities, but also in Deming and Farmington and Kingman and Bisbee. Now the morning air was cool and clear and calm in appearance only: the dawn lit up a landscape being bombarded with signals. Now the revolution could reach high gear. By 1985, ninety-eight percent of all American homes had at least one television set.

On the ground, meanwhile, the two-lane U.S. highways of the first half-century evolved into the interstate system of super-highways. In Illinois a man named Ray Kroc developed a chain of hamburger stores called McDonald's, thus becoming the Henry Ford of food merchandising. The DC-3s, beneath which the mesas, buttes, and peaks had crept at an almost scenic rate, gave way to jet aircraft that could carry 150 people—and later 250—clear across the Southwest in less than two hours at 37,000 feet.

Suddenly the Southwest was as accessible—maybe more so—to a television advertiser or to a McDonald's site selector as a neighborhood in New York or Los Angeles.

The same products were advertised and made available from coast to coast. The evening news sounded the same in New York, Peoria, Gallup, and Los Angeles. Even local newscasters sounded alike. It was obvious that, to be taken seriously on television, local newscasters all had to sound like Yankees. Talk shows fed out information that sounded vaguely like social issues. It was impossible, in this country, to get away from "Donohue." Then, in 1990, along came truly global television. As former *New York Times* reporter and author David Halberstam said, "The world is wired for sound." People in ShowLow knew as much, and as quickly, about Soviet politics and the stock market and "good" and "bad" cholesterol as people in Chicago.

People started to talk about a "homogenizing" effect that would spread across the nation in the wake of the information revolution. They feared the loss of the regionality that for more than a century had informed the various corners and middle geography of the continent with distinct personalities. Where once there had been a Northeast and a South and a Midwest and a Southwest, after the Great Homogenization there would be only Anyplace, U.S.A., one latitude culturally indistinguishable from another.

I heard that talk, and understood it intellectually, but I didn't put it on the ground until one summer day in, of all places, the deep Southwest. We were passing through Santa Clara, in the red-rock country of southwestern Utah. I asked a gas jockey where was the best place to eat in town, thinking he would direct us to some picturesque cafe serving grub particular to southwestern Utah.

"Well, there's a Wendy's over in Saint George," said the gas jockey. As I stared at him, I got a mental image of a Wendy's at the foot of every third exit off Interstate 40, from Los Angeles to Knoxville. In a flash of horror, I saw the Pink Adobe in Santa Fe bought out by Red Lobster. I saw the extinction of sopaipillas. I saw a commercial introducing the McChimichanga. I remembered a line from a song, about Indians dressed up like cowboys, and cowboys putting on turquoise and leather. Pretty soon they'd all be dressing like Bo Jackson. It was awful. But it was possible.

From that day, I started to look for signs of the approaching homogenization. It was visible everywhere. The mall is merely an outlet for homogenization. There may be two or three regional department stores in a mall, but all the other stores are the same. Inside a mall, you can be in Phoenix or Minneapolis. Kids in malls all dress alike and have all begun to sound alike. In Texas, when I was growing up, we thought that everything new started in California and took about two years to reach us. That interval is now down to about twenty seconds, and in fact has begun to run the other way.

That is where the Southwest comes in. There are signs that the Great Homogenization may be halted by the cultural and spiritual boundaries of the Southwest. The possibility also exists that the ancient wellsprings which feed that culture and spirit could become the basis for a new national mythology. If information can be delivered into a region, it can be delivered out. The result in the 1970s and 1980s has been the rotating in-ness of regional identities. New York and Los Angeles urbanites are always in, and viewers never seem to weary of cops and car chases. For the longest time, disco and its culture was in. Then lately Texas has been in, and Cajun has been in, and Southern women have been in, and Lake Woebegone has been in, leading the way for any information having to do with small-town in-ness. As the 1990s began, the Southwest came in: southwestern food and design showed up in the most cosmopolitan enclaves and, naturally, on fast-food menus.

Part of this in-ness process is simply a reaction to the revolution. Faced with the prospect of nothing to eat but Wendyburgers, people—especially older folks—go overboard to reestablish their regional identities. The younger folks, members of the first fully urbanized generation in American history, all think and dress like Californians already and don't know any different.

But another part of the process looks like sampling. Americans have vast new access to themselves. They respond to the rotating in-ness like people willing to try things out, looking for something that will work. This comes, not coincidentally, at a time when Americans feel at a loss for some unifying theme. Government bureaucracy, a feeble economy, the corporate greed of the eighties, the S & L failures, drugs, crime, pollution, and homelessness all contribute to the national pessimism: What is wrong, here? Doesn't anything about this country work anymore?

The thirst for unity became apparent with the Persian Gulf conflict. United States material and technology were at the heart of an allied force that waged a short and extremely efficient war against Iraq. Americans saw it all on CNN, with galvanic effect. The American military machine worked very well, thank you, and the response was more than enthusiastic. It was affectionate; it was unifying. The people tied a yellow ribbon around the entire country.

Of course the trade-offs are too severe for war to work as an ongoing national mythology. But the lingering lesson from the Persian Gulf is that Americans crave a new national mythology, if only they could find one that would work, in a technological world that the late Joseph Campbell described as thoroughly "demythologized."

Campbell was not quite right. Mythologies abound in this country, but at a state or regional level. As a Texan, I am fully aware, though I can't explain it, of a Texas mythology with which Texans strongly identify. Arizonans, New Mexicans, Coloradoans, and Utahans all have similar feelings. I have thought that if somehow the Texas mythology could be expanded across the entire country, then that would be the kind of national mythology we are talking about. I don't think that particular idea would work. In fact I shudder, in spite of myself, at the notion of

187

an entire nation of Texans. It wouldn't work because the Texas mythology, or the Arizona mythology or the New Mexico mythology, is not fundamental enough to underpin a nation.

We can take clues from those mythologies, though, because they are political sections of a larger mythology; they are cut out like cookies from the bigger ball of dough. They all have to do with place. And the place we all share is right here at our feet.

An Earth movement was under way long before the recent focus on the Southwest. An awareness was growing that, to save ourselves, we had to save the planet. The way to do that, apparently, was to organize, to protest, and to call for environmental laws to be passed. But laws are an unsatisfactory substitute for a way of life. Lawyers might indeed save the planet, but who would care to live in such an arid cultural landscape?

Then the Southwest became in. Native Americans became in. For the Earth movement, they may have acted like the Santa Clara gas jockey, putting intellectual matters on the ground. In watching the hunter's ritual in *Dances With Wolves*, in reading Tony Hillerman's stories woven from Navajo life, in responding to the instinctive pull of the land so prevalent in Southwestern art and architecture, Americans may have noticed a vague harmony rising. It is the harmony many of them acknowledge in God's fashioning Adam from clay, and in their acceptance of lives lived, dust unto dust. From the earth we came, and to the earth we will return. What was missing, though, was the harmony in between. Residents of the technological world haven't given much thought to their natural partnership with Earth. The Earth gods have noticed this, and thrown up greenhouse effects, ozone holes, acid rains, droughts, famines, and other signals telling the people that,

without a little harmony restoration here, the day soon will arrive when enough is enough.

Curious, that at this particular time there should emerge in the popular culture a beautiful place where the landscape is so dominant and whose native residents have for centuries been developing a model for living in harmony with that landscape. Sure, aspects of Southwestern culture became commercial; the cuisine was trendy; and "Santa Fe architecture" became a buzzword in the slick, heavy, lifestyle-of-the-rich magazines. But apparently the national scrutiny has gone beyond the obvious. The same signals of harmony that for decades have attracted artists and thinkers to the Southwest, began in the nineties to reach the masses. The process is still new, and it still takes imagination to see a twenty-first-century America rooting its values in an Earth mythology. People might scoff at the idea of big government and big business giving the slightest recognition to such principles. But the mythology is older and bigger than government and business. Elsewhere in these pages is an argument that this old mythology has entered its own cycle of rebirth. It is an idea whose time has come again, with, to paraphrase Victor Hugo, a tread greater than mighty armies.

No greater symbol of harmony exists than a circle closing. A century ago the westward European migration routinely wrested from Native Americans the land that they held holy. Now the Europeans, looking through those same Native American eyes, are starting to believe that the land is holy, and that the people, the beasts, the forests, the clouds, and the rain are all its children. What an irony, if the time has come when the Indians help the white man win back the land.

BIBLIOGRAPHY

Arnberger, Leslie P. *Flowers of the Southwest Mountains*. Tucson: Southwest Parks and Monuments Association, 1982.

Barnes, F.A. *Utah Canyon Country*. Salt Lake City: Utah Geographic Series, Inc., 1986.

Brugge, David M. *Navahos in the Catholic Church: Records of New Mexico 1694–1875*. Tsaile: Navajo Community College Press, 1985.

Casey, Robert L. *Journey to the High Southwest*. Third edition, Boston: Globe Pequot, 1988.

Clark, Kenneth. *Civilization*. New York: Harper & Row, 1969.

Forest, Earle R. *Missions & Pueblos of the Old Southwest*. Reprint of 1929 edition. Rio Grande, 1983.

Ganci, Dave. *Desert Hiking*. Twenty-second edition, Wilderness Press, 1988.

Grattan, Virginia L. *Mary Colter, Builder Upon the Red Earth*. Flagstaff: Northland Press, 1980.

Hallon, W. Eugene. *The Southwest: Old & New*. University of Nebraska Press, 1968.

Hathaway, Nancy. *Native American Portraits: 1862–1918*. San Francisco: Chronicle Books, 1990.

Hillerman, Tony. *Hillerman Country*. New York: HarperCollins Publishers, 1991.

Historic Trading Posts. Flagstaff: Museum of Northern Arizona, 1991.

Houlihan, Patrick, Jerold L. Collings, Sarah Nestor, and Jonathan Batkin. *Harmony by Hand*. San Francisco: Chronicle Books, 1987.

Hughes, J. Donald. *In the House of Stone and Light: A Human History of the Grand Canyon*. Denver: University of Denver, 1978.

Hyde, Philip. *Drylands: The Deserts of North America*. San Diego: Harcourt Brace Jovanovich, 1987.

Jones, Dewitt. *Canyon Country*. Portland: Graphic Arts Center Publishing Company, 1986.

Lavender, David. *One Man's West*. Lincoln: University of Nebraska Press, 1977.

Lesure, Thomas B. *All the Southwest*. Second edition, Allsport Publishing.

Lister, Robert H. and Florence C. Lister. *Those Who Came Before: Southwestern Archeology in the National Park System*. Tucson: The University of Arizona Press, 1983.

Mahood, Ruth I., editor. *Photographer of the Southwest: Adam Clark Vroman, 1856–1916*. Introduction by Beaumont Newhall. New York: Bonanza Books, 1961.

McPhee, John. *Outcroppings*. Layton, Utah: Gibbs Smith, 1988.

Muench, David. *Desert Images*. New York: Harcourt Brace Jovanovich, 1979.

Nelson, Mary Carroll. *Masters of Western Art*. New York: Watson-Guptill Publications, 1982.

Olin, George. *Mammals of the Southwest Deserts*. Tucson: Southwest Parks and Monuments Association, 1982.

Parks, Stephen. *R.C. Gorman: A Portrait*. Boston: Little, Brown and Company, 1983.

Pike, Donald G. *Anasazi, Ancient People of the Rock*. New York: Harmony Books, 1974.

Running, John. *Honor Dance: Native American Photographs*. Reno: University of Nevada Press, 1985.

Schaafsma, Polly. *The Rock Art of Utah*. Cambridge: Harvard University, 1971.

Schmidt, Jeremy. *The Rockies: Backbone of a Continent*. New York: Thunder Bay Press-Abbeville Press, 1990.

———. *Adventuring in the Rockies*. San Francisco: Sierra Club Books, 1986.

Till, Tom. *Colorado: Images From Above*. Englewood: Westcliffe Publishers, Inc., 1987.

192

American Southwest:
A People and Their Landscape
produced in association with the publisher by
McQuiston & Partners, Inc. in Del Mar, California:
art direction, Don McQuiston;
design, Don McQuiston and Joyce Sweet;
editing, Julie Olfe;
composition, Tom Lewis, Inc.; text type, Goudy Old Style;
printed in Hong Kong by Dai Nippon Printing Co., Ltd.

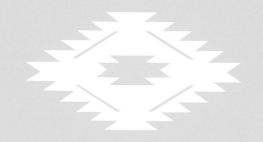